ARE YOU AFRAID OF DEATH? DON'T BE!

THERE IS AN ESCAPE — THERE IS A WAY OUT

JOHN 11:25-26

Jim Taylor

Taylor/New Harbor Press
1601 Mt. Rushmore Rd, Ste 3288
Rapid City, SD 57701
www.newharborpress.com

Are You Afraid of Death? Don't Be!/Jim Taylor —1st ed.
ISBN 978-1-63357-481-6

The American Standard Bible is used for all scripture references in this book. The reason for that is because the American Standard Bible is the King James Version; it is not another new translation but a revision of the King James Version itself. The American Standard Revisers viewed each word the King James committee used in their translation and they considered how a word might have changed in over a 250 year period, and if so they tried to find a more accurate word to use. There were no major changes in the two versions. The King James Version is in the opinion of many—including the opinion of this author—the most accurate translation of the original documents into the English language. Below is one of the changes the American Standard translators made.

For the whole house of Ahab shall perish: and I will cut off from Ahab him that pisseth against the wall, and him that is shut up and left in Israel: (2 Kings 9:8) KJV

For the whole house of Ahab shall perish; and I will cut off from Ahab every man-child, and him that is shut up and him that is left at large in Israel. (2 Kings 9:8). ASV

Other Books by Jim Taylor

REVELATION TO JOHN'S APOCALYPSE UNVEILED AND REVEALED

The Spiritual View of a Carnal War

LEVITICUS UNVEILED AND REVEALED

The Lamb and the Altar — the Lamb of God and the Cross

THE POWER OF THE CROSS UNVEILED AND REVEALED IN JESUS

One Man Sinned and All Men Died, another Man Died So All Might Live

ALMIGHTY JEHOVAH GOD UNVEILED AND REVEALED IN JESUS

HEBREWS UNVEILED AND REVEALED

Leviticus Fulfilled by the Coming of Jesus

I AM

I Am Jehovah, Covenant God of Israel —I Am Jesus, Covenant God of Christians

JESUS

The Perfect Man—The Fullness of God

Contents

Preface

GOD CREATED THE WORLD in six days and He rested on the seventh (Genesis 2:1-2). It was on the sixth day of the creation He made a man, and He called him Adam (Genesis 2:7). He put Adam into a deep sleep and He took a woman from his side, and she became Adam's wife (Genesis 2:20-25) and she was called Eve. (There was an occasion when a young woman who was married to her young husband—they had not been married long—and she had not been treated by her husband with the respect she deserved. She was offended, and justly so. Her reply was, "Listen mister, I was not taken from beneath your feet, I was taken from your side and from under your arm!")

The reason God created the world and brought Adam and Eve into his creation is because he wanted children to love; for God is love. John wrote, "Beloved, let us love one another: for love is of God; and every one that loveth is begotten of God, and knoweth God. He that loveth not knoweth not God; for God is love" (1 John 4:7-8). For even the almighty God to have his love fulfilled He must have someone to love. Therefore, God did not create the world so he would have children to love him, though he desires that infinitely; God created the world because he wanted children to love, and He loved them so much he gave them his world, and He gave them complete control of all things in it. Moses wrote,

> And God said, Let us make man in our image, after our likeness: and let them have dominion over the fish of the sea, and over the birds of the heavens, and over the cattle, and over all the earth, and over every creeping thing that creepeth upon the earth. And God created man in his own image, in the image of God created he him; male and female created he them. And God blessed them: and God said unto them, Be fruitful, and multiply, and replenish the earth, and subdue it; and have dominion over the fish of the sea, and over the birds of the heavens, and over every living thing that moveth upon the earth. (Genesis 1:26-28)

All that Adam and Eve had to do to please God was to abide in his garden, dress it and keep it, bring children into the world, and be obedient to their heavenly Father. God gave them one simple law that they were to obey and in doing so their obedience to that law would establish their love and their faithfulness to their Father.

> And Jehovah God took the man, and put him into the garden of Eden to dress it and to keep it. And Jehovah God commanded the man, saying, Of every tree of the garden thou mayest freely eat: but of the tree of the knowledge of good and evil, thou shalt not eat of it: for in the day that thou eatest thereof thou shalt surely die. (Genesis 2:15-17)

How simple it was: God's children had the most beautiful place to live that was possible, they had food abundantly, and they had perfect fellowship with their Father. How much better could it get? What a wonderful place with the Father His children occupy when they have been given life from the Almighty just because He wanted children to love, and they have been given that life in the image of their heavenly Father.

A person might wonder: if God created children to be the objects of His love, why do so many of them fall into great temptations and frightening traumas that threaten them in many ways? God's love is seen in his constant care and protection of his children; but how much greater does His love appear when it is his love that delivers his children out of frightening dangers that are so severe they threaten the loss of their possessions, the loss of their health, and even the loss of their lives?

There was a man who learned that lesson by experience, his name was Job. Job was a man who loved and respected God so much that he kept himself free from sin at all cost (Job 1:1, 22). He even offered sacrifices for his children in case they might have sin charged against them (Job 1:4-5). Job's pure life threatened Satan, and Satan appeared before God and told Him that the only reason Job served Him so steadfastly was for what he could get out of it. It is written in Job,

> Now it came to pass on the day when the sons of God came to present themselves before Jehovah, that Satan also came among them. And Jehovah said unto Satan, Whence comest thou? Then Satan answered Jehovah, and said, From going to and fro in the earth, and from walking up and down in it. And Jehovah said unto Satan, Hast thou considered my servant Job? for there is none like him in the earth, a perfect and an upright man, one that feareth God, and turneth away from evil.

> Then Satan answered Jehovah, and said, Doth Job fear God for nought? Hast not thou made a hedge about him, and about his house, and about all that he hath, on every side? thou hast blessed the work of his hands, and his substance is increased in the land. But put forth thy hand now, and touch all that he hath, and he will renounce thee to thy face. And Jehovah said unto Satan, Behold, all that he hath is in thy power; only upon himself put not forth thy hand. So Satan went forth from the presence of Jehovah. (Job 1:6-12)

God allowed Satan to tempt Job by taking away all of his possessions and even his children. Satan immediately went to work on Job and tried his best to cause Job to deny God and sin. In a just a moment Job suffered more than most men suffer in a lifetime. It is written in Job,

> And it fell on a day when his sons and his daughters were eating and drinking wine in their eldest brother's house, that there came a messenger unto Job, and said, The oxen were plowing, and the asses feeding beside them; and the Sabeans fell upon them, and took them away: yea, they have slain the servants with the edge of the sword; and I only am escaped alone to tell thee. While he was yet speaking, there came also another, and said, The fire of God is fallen from heaven, and hath burned up the sheep and the servants, and consumed them; and I only am escaped alone to tell thee. While he was yet speaking, there came also another, and said, The Chaldeans made three bands, and fell upon the camels, and have taken them away, yea, and slain the servants with the

> edge of the sword; and I only am escaped alone to tell thee. While he was yet speaking, there came also another, and said, Thy sons and thy daughters were eating and drinking wine in their eldest brother's house; and, behold, there came a great wind from the wilderness, and smote the four corners of the house, and it fell upon the young men, and they are dead; and I only am escaped alone to tell thee. Then Job arose, and rent his robe, and shaved his head, and fell down upon the ground, and worshipped; and he said, Naked came I out of my mother's womb, and naked shall I return thither: Jehovah gave, and Jehovah hath taken away; blessed be the name of Jehovah. In all this Job sinned not, nor charged God foolishly. (Job 1:13-22)

What we see here is the power Satan has to tempt and destroy unless he is prohibited from such evil exploits by the Almighty. Satan has the power to tempt people and bring them to the depths of despair, and without God's protection that is what Satan would do to everyone who believed in God. Through this entire incident Job remained faithful and steadfast to the Lord even after he had lost all of his possessions and even his children.

Satan appeared before God a second time and he told God that if Job lost his health he would deny his Maker, and God allowed Satan to destroy Job's health until he was at the door of death. It is written in Job,

> And Jehovah said unto Satan, Hast thou considered my servant Job? for there is none like him in the earth, a perfect and an upright man, one that feareth God, and turneth away from evil:

> and he still holdeth fast his integrity, although thou movedst me against him, to destroy him without cause. And Satan answered Jehovah, and said, Skin for skin, yea, all that a man hath will he give for his life. And Jehovah said unto Satan, Behold, he is in thy hand; only spare his life. So Satan went forth from the presence of Jehovah, and smote Job with sore boils from the sole of his foot unto his crown. And he took him a potsherd to scrape himself therewith; and he sat among the ashes. Then said his wife unto him, Dost thou still hold fast thine integrity? renounce God, and die. But he said unto her, Thou speakest as one of the foolish women speaketh. What? shall we receive good at the hand of God, and shall we not receive evil? In all this did not Job sin with his lips. (Job 2:3-13)

Job remained faithful and steadfast to the Almighty and he refused to accuse Him for causing his suffering. God rewarded him by giving him back his health, his children, and twice the number of possessions he originally had. In Job's letter it is written,

> And Jehovah turned the captivity of Job, when he prayed for his friends: and Jehovah gave Job twice as much as he had before. Then came there unto him all his brethren, and all his sisters, and all they that had been of his acquaintance before, and did eat bread with him in his house: and they bemoaned him, and comforted him concerning all the evil that Jehovah had brought upon him: every man also gave him a piece of money, and every one a ring of gold. So Jehovah blessed the latter end of Job more than his beginning: And he

> had fourteen thousand sheep, and six thousand camels, and a thousand yoke of oxen, and a thousand she-asses. He had also seven sons and three daughters. And he called the name of the first, Jemimah: and the name of the second Keziah; and the name of the third, Keren-happuch. And in all the land were no women found so fair as the daughters of Job: and their father gave them inheritance among their brethren. And after this Job lived a hundred and forty years, and saw his sons, and his sons' sons, so Job died, being old and full of days. (Job 42:10-17)

A Christian must wonder why God would allow Satan to tempt a man so severely just because that man loved God, feared God, and was exceedingly faithful to God. It seems at first that such action borders on cruelty, but not so! First, Satan challenged God and told Him that the only reason His children served Him was for what they could get out of it for themselves. God said that is not so. Satan said, "Prove it, I can prove what I am saying to you is true." Thus God allowed Satan to have his way with Job, but Job stood steadfast in his love and faith and he would not deny his Maker. This was a time when it was God who had faith in a man and at the same time that man had faith in his Maker.

Job is the man who humiliated Satan and brought him down, and he proved that men of faith can conquer the evil one and take away his power. But there is more: Job is the example to the faithful that when they love God, trust God, and are faithful to God—but they suffer greatly in spite of their love and loyalty anyway— it is not because God has forsaken them or quit loving them, it is to give them a way to conquer the evil one and be greatly rewarded by the Almighty for having done so. When men resist Satan they conquer him by not yielding to his temptations, and temptation is the only power he has, and he is forced to just leave them alone. James wrote,

> But he giveth more grace. Wherefore the scripture saith, God resisteth the proud, but giveth grace to the humble. Be subject therefore unto God; but resist the devil, and he will flee from you. Draw nigh to God, and he will draw nigh to you. Cleanse your hands, ye sinners; and purify your hearts, ye doubleminded. (James 4:7-8)

The reason the devil flees from the one who resists him is because he does not like being humiliated, and that is exactly what Job did; he resisted the devil, the devil fled from him, and the Almighty drew him into his arms and gave him the world.

The only power Satan has is temptation, and when one yields to his temptation they sin, and they die. However, when one does not yield to temptation they overcome and they live, and that is something Satan cannot stand. When Jesus abolished death, and even the fear of death by his cross and resurrection, he took away all the power Satan had (Hebrews 2:14-15).

As strange as it might seem it was the love of God that allowed Job to be tempted so severely that he was brought to the depths of despair. The power of God's love was exemplified even greater when Job overcame his sufferings and God established him as a pillar of the faithful, and he was greatly rewarded for his faith. Job is the example to God's children who suffer in many ways, that no matter how greatly they suffer they shall always be protected by the Almighty and they shall always overcome—if they remain faithful. When they overcome they shall be stronger and better off than they were before they were tempted, and it is Job who is the proof that such is true. Paul wrote, "There hath no temptation taken you but such as man can bear: but God is faithful, who will not suffer you to be tempted above that ye are able; but will with the temptation make also the way of escape, that ye may be able to endure it" (1 Corinthians 10:13).

If Job had not had this terrible experience he would have just been another man of great faith and possessions who would have been soon forgotten after he left this world—but Job will never be forgotten! In Ezekiel it is written,

> And the word of Jehovah came unto me, saying, Son of man, when a land sinneth against me by committing a trespass, and I stretch out my hand upon it, and break the staff of the bread thereof, and send famine upon it, and cut off from it man and beast; though these three men, Noah, Daniel, and Job, were in it, they should deliver but their own souls by their righteousness, saith the Lord Jehovah. If I cause evil beasts to pass through the land, and they ravage it, and it be made desolate, so that no man may pass through because of the beasts; though these three men were in it, as I live, saith the Lord Jehovah, they should deliver neither sons nor daughters; they only should be delivered, but the land should be desolate. Or if I bring a sword upon that land, and say, Sword, go through the land; so that I cut off from it man and beast; though these three men were in it, as I live, saith the Lord Jehovah, they should deliver neither sons nor daughters, but they only should be delivered themselves. Or if I send a pestilence into that land, and pour out my wrath upon it in blood, to cut off from it man and beast; though Noah, Daniel, and Job, were in it, as I live, saith the Lord Jehovah, they should deliver neither son nor daughter; they should but deliver their own souls by their righteousness. (Ezekiel 14:12-20)

James wrote, "Take, brethren, for an example of suffering and of patience, the prophets who spake in the name of the Lord. Behold, we call them blessed that endured: ye have heard of the patience of Job, and have seen the end of the Lord, how that the Lord is full of pity, and merciful" (James 5:10-11).

The example of Job is a rich lesson to all those who suffer severe temptations, even to the point of death. When a Christian is tempted and falls into the same sorrows as Job experienced, they should not blame God for their sorrows, and they should not feel it is because God has forsaken them, or quit loving them; they should see it is an opportunity of something to conquer and overcome just as Job overcame, and it takes great faith to achieve that.

When God created the world sin and death did not exist, those evil forces came into the world by the transgression of one man, Adam, who disobeyed the Almighty and fell. Sin is lawlessness (1 John 3:4); sin is disobedience to God by breaking his commandments and His heart (Genesis 6:5-8), and the penalty for such insubordination is death. The first sin was committed when Satan tempted Eve to eat the fruit of God's tree. When she was deceived and overcome with temptation she yielded to the impulse and she ate, and she sinned; and then Adam also ate the fruit of God's forbidden tree, and he sinned

That act of disobedience condemned Adam, Eve, Satan, and the entire creation, and it was that moment the appointment of death was established for all men and the creation was subjected to vanity. It is written in the Hebrew letter, "And inasmuch as it is appointed unto men once to die, and after this cometh judgment; so Christ also, having been once offered to bear the sins of many, shall appear a second time, apart from sin, to them that wait for him, unto salvation" (Hebrews 9:27-28). Paul wrote,

> For the creation was subjected to vanity, not of its own will, but by reason of him who subjected

> it, in hope that the creation itself also shall be delivered from the bondage of corruption into the liberty of the glory of the children of God. For we know that the whole creation groaneth and travaileth in pain together until now" (Romans 8:20-22).

It was Adam's transgression that corrupted the creation and caused it be subjected to vanity and brought death into God's perfect world. Romans 5:12-21 establishes that fact beyond the shadow of a doubt. Viewing the first part of each verse in Romans 5:12-21 sums up the message of doom that was caused by Adam's trespass: "Therefore, as through one man sin entered into the world, and death through sin; and so death passed unto all men, for that all sinned" (v12); "For if by the trespass of the one the many died...." (v15); "...for the judgment came of one unto condemnation..." (v16); "For if, by the trespass of the one, death reigned through the one..." (v17); "So then as through one trespass the judgment came unto all men to condemnation..." (v18); "For as through the one man's disobedience the many were made sinners..." (v19). From this it is very clear that it was just one trespass, and only one trespass, or Adam's sin that condemned the creation and caused the reign of death.

It was Jesus' sacrifice on the cross that annulled Adam's trespass and abolished its consequence, which is death. By summing up the message of the second part of those verses we see the power of Jesus and his cross to annul Adam's sin and cancel its consequences: They declare "...much more did the grace of God, and the gift by the grace of the one man, Jesus Christ, abound unto the many" (v15); "...but the free gift came of many trespasses unto justification." (V16); "...much more shall they that receive the abundance of grace and of the gift of righteousness reign in life through the one, even Jesus Christ (v17); "...even so through one act of righteousness the free gift came unto all men to justification of life (v18); "...even so through the obedience of the one shall the many be made righteous" (v19). Why is it so difficult to put those verses together as they are written and accept them for what they say? Doing that declares that just as it was one act of disobedience that condemned the creation, so also it was only one act of righteousness, or the Cross, that immediately annulled Adam's sin, restored the creation back to its original perfection, set all men free from law, sin, condemnation, and death; and gave all men eternal life—if they will accept it. Jesus summed all of this up very well when he said to Martha, "Jesus said unto her, I am the resurrection, and the life: he that believeth on me, though he die, yet shall he live; and whosoever liveth and believeth on me shall never die. Believest thou this?" (John 11:25–26).

God keeps his promises and his commandments, and once a sin had been committed He had but one of two choices to make—He must either condemn the sinner and the creation as he said he would do, or He must make a way to forgive the sinner and redeem the creation. God loved his world so much he chose the second way, but at infinite cost to himself and to the Word—who Himself is God (John 1:1-2). For God to redeem the world that had fallen, the Almighty himself must leave the Godhead by being born to a virgin and become a man. It is the Word, who is God, who must leave the Godhead to become the Son of man and the Son of God, and He would live a perfect life without sin until he was about thirty years of age. Then he would offer his life from a cross as a human sacrifice that would take away Adam's sin and all the sins of the world (John 1:29). It was Adam's act of insubordination that condemned the world, and it was Jesus' infinite act of obedience that restored the creation back to God in its original glory and holiness, and greater, and God had to become a man to accomplish that (Hebrews 2:14-16).

Adam's sin immediately brought condemnation upon all men, and that condemnation was the appointment with death that fell upon the entire creation. It is written in the Hebrew letter, "And inasmuch as it is appointed unto men once to die, and after this cometh judgment; so Christ also, having been once offered to bear the sins of many, shall appear a second time, apart from sin, to them that wait for him, unto salvation" (Hebrews 9:27-28). The very verse that states that men were appointed to death because of Adam's sin also reveals the way out of it; that way out is Christ who came to take away Adam's sin and all sin, and restore righteousness. John wrote, "On the morrow he seeth Jesus coming unto him, and saith, Behold, the Lamb of God, that taketh away the sin of the world!" John also wrote,

> If we say that we have fellowship with him and walk in the darkness, we lie, and do not the truth: but if we walk in the light, as he is in the light, we have fellowship one with another, and the blood of Jesus his Son cleanseth us from all sin. If we say that we have no sin, we deceive ourselves, and the truth is not in us. (1 John 1:6-8)

Once a person understands that all their sins have been forgiven by the blood of Jesus and his death on the cross, and his resurrection, they should also understand that they no longer face death, or the fear of death; for when there is no sin, there is no death, and when there is no death, there can be no fear of death.

Therefore, death does not exist in the Christian world, and Jesus himself said that, just as John wrote, "I am the resurrection, and the life: he that believeth on me, though he die, yet shall he live; and whosoever liveth and believeth on me shall never die. Believest thou this?" (John 11:25-26). All who have lived in the faith as believers of God, but have died, shall live again—and all those who are still alive and live in that faith shall never die. This means all who live in the Holy Faith shall never see death, for in the Christian world death does not exist, it is called a *sleep*. Matthew wrote, "and the tombs were opened; and many bodies of the saints that had fallen asleep were raised" (Matthew 27:52). Luke wrote, "And they stoned Stephen, calling upon the Lord, and saying, Lord Jesus, receive my spirit. And he kneeled down, and cried with a loud voice, Lord, lay not this sin to their charge. And when he had said this, he fell asleep" (Acts 7:59-60). What a powerful force it was that allowed a man who was suffering greatly by being stoned—stoned by having large rocks hurled upon him the size of grapefruit until he was dead and he was covered with stones—and then suddenly awake in the same moment to find himself in the most beautiful place he could ever imagine, and he would live in that home forever. There is coming the day when Stephan's body shall also live again forever, and in a new world.

One of the most horrible pains anyone can experience is losing a loved one, and that loss is called death. It is a man losing his wife, a wife losing her husband, or parents losing a child. Such grief and pain seems almost impossible to bear, and there is no way to escape those feelings. Even the animal world falls into this condemnation. There are animals such as wolves, swans, geese, eagles, parrots and many others that mate for life, and most of them will only mate once. If they lose their mate they grieve terribly, and some of them grieve themselves even unto death. What a powerful force death is! But if a person can understand that when they lose a precious loved one to death their loved one has not died at all; they have just fallen asleep—It might be a long, long sleep, but nevertheless it is a sleep—and it is not forever. The person who is left knows that one day they shall be with their loved one again, and that helps relieve the heartache. Christ is the answer to all of our tribulations.

Death is very real and the fear of death is very painful. That is the reason the Son of God came into the world; He came to abolish death and take away its fear. The Hebrew writer said, "Since then the children are sharers in flesh and blood, he also himself in like manner partook of the same; that through death he might bring to nought him that had the power of death, that is, the devil; and might deliver all them who through fear of death were all their lifetime subject to bondage" (Hebrews 2:14-16).

The pain a person experiences by losing a loved one is caused by knowing they shall not see their mate again in this world. One example of how painful death is when two people who have walked together, talked together, ate together, slept together and had beautiful a relationship with each other for many years: and then in just an instant one of them is gone. The one who is left experiences a feeling that is so sad and so lonely it cannot be explained—it can only be felt. Then the presence of loved one who fell asleep is replaced by the horrible feeling of sorrow and loneliness. However, that pain can be relieved by prayer and by believing the promises of Jesus—that the person who left did not die; they just went home to be with their Father and their church family that had gone on before them. Relief comes to the one who is left by knowing that someday they to shall to pass into that same world to be with their loved one again, and forever. Death is going to happen and there is no way out of it except to believe in Christ and his promises, and Jesus and his promises are most certain and very real.

I read of a man who had been married to the same woman for many years. She was old, ill, and her husband was holding her when she *fell asleep*. His last words to her, as he was crying and as his children were with him were, "Honey, call me home." His children said they would never forget those words. It was "*Honey*" who called her husband home just twenty-eight days later, a true blessing from God. The old man who was holding his dying mate and crying was just experiencing a natural emotion that only humans have. Why do we do that? Animals mourn and grieve but they do not shed tears. Some have said real men don't cry. Not so! Crying should be viewed as a natural way of relieving great emotional pain and agony that can be alleviated no other way, and men are not exempt. Laughing that is caused by experiencing great happiness and joy can cause tears; it can cause one to cry just as a horrible experience of great pain can cause one to cry. In any case laughing and crying are emotional experiences that no one should try to restrain.

There was an occasion when President Eisenhower was being interviewed about his experiences being the commander of the military forces during World War Two. He was asked a question about Normandy, and Ike became very quiet. Then he became emotional and he wept. He was the commander of men he loved, and they loved him, and he knew when they were chosen to invade the Normandy beaches many of them would die, and he did not take that lightly. If General, then President Eisenhower wept, and if Jesus wept, then crying cannot be a sign of weakness, it is a demonstration of strength and compassion.

There was a little boy, he was about eleven or twelve, and he noticed that his father never cried when everyone else was crying. His father had a caring face of concern but no tears. That little boy had a little dog, and he loved it like a brother. The little dog died, and when his mom and dad told him his little dog had gone to heaven, he broke up and started crying uncontrollably, and his mother was crying with him. He looked up at his father and he saw a big tear running down his cheek from his right eye. The little boy's sister also noticed that her father never cried. But she said when her grandmother died, her father's mother, he had a big tear in his eye. I feel so sorry for people who can't or won't cry.

There was a beautiful young woman who lost her husband to death. After the funeral when they were in the cemetery, and her husband was about to be lowered into the ground, she became highly emotional and started crying. Her friends tried to comfort her by hugging her and saying, honey don't cry, its ok, don't cry. There was another friend of both her and her husband, and he just took hold of her and pulled her closely to him and he said, honey, you just put your head on my shoulder and you cry until you just can't cry anymore, and I will put on a dry shirt.

When a person dies, and they are a Christian, they just meet the appointment Adam made for them by his original sin, and they leave this world of suffering, anxiety, grief, pain and uncertainty—and they go home to the eternal world of glory where death does not exist.

Death, as it is called, must happen for a person escape this world and enter the next, and that is why Paul called death a victory; death is our only escape from this world into the next. There were only two men who did not experience Adam's appointment with death; they were Enoch, the seventh from Adam (Genesis 5:21-24), and the prophet Elijah (2 Kings 2:11-12). But without Christ there is no reason to view death as a victory. Paul wrote,

> Now this I say, brethren, that flesh and blood cannot inherit the kingdom of God; neither doth corruption inherit incorruption. Behold, I tell you a mystery: We all shall not sleep, but we shall all be changed, in a moment, in the twinkling of an eye, at the last trump: for the trumpet shall sound, and the dead shall be raised incorruptible, and we shall be changed. For this corruptible must put on incorruption, and this mortal must put on immortality. But when this corruptible shall have put on incorruption, and this mortal shall have put on immortality, then shall come to pass the saying that is written, Death is swallowed up in victory. O death, where is thy victory? O death, where is thy sting? The sting of death is sin; and the power of sin is the law: but thanks be to God,

> who giveth us the victory through our Lord Jesus Christ. (1 Corinthians 15:50-57)

When Christ was resurrected from the tomb he destroyed sin, and with sin he destroyed death, and therefore, for the person of the faith there is no such thing as death, it just doesn't exist. It takes great faith to see that and believe it, and it takes great faith to attend a memorial service for one who has died, and all that is of left of them is a little box of their ashes; and believe those ashes shall live again and become the body of the person who died. But if we believe in Jesus and we believe he is real, and if we believe the Bible to be the Word of God, then we know His promises are true.

I read of an actress who many years ago played in many movies. She was beautiful and well behaved, and she played only the parts in movies that were of high moral caricature, such as no bad language and no bedroom scenes—but she had more than a tremendous fear of death. If only she could have been taught that there is a way out of death what a relief she could have had; and she is not the only one who has that feeling of fear.

Jesus is our only way out of death, he is our only access to the Father, and he is our only hope of leaving death and entering the kingdom of heaven. Jesus said, "I am the way, and the truth, and the life: no one cometh unto the Father, but by me" (John 14:6). He also said "I am the resurrection, and the life: he that believeth on me, though he die, yet shall he live; and whosoever liveth and believeth on me shall never die. Believest thou this?" (John 11:25-26).

There are many people who have the same tremendous fear of death that this actress had, but if they can be taught, or if they will read the Bible, they can see that there is an escape, and that there is a way out of death forever, and what an infinite relief it is to know that. If we can believe that Jesus is real and that he truly is the Son of God; that He lived some thirty-three years on this earth as a man who could work miracles; that his purpose in coming into the world was to give his life on a cross to abolish death and take away sin; then we can believe his promises. Jesus promised us that he will deliver us out of the king of terrors, as Job called it (Job 18:14), and into his kingdom. Therefore instead of Christians fearing death and looking at it as the king of terrors, as did Job, they should view it as the only way they have to exit this present evil world of sin and suffering, and the only way they have of entering the glorious and perfect kingdom of God where not even the least little thing can go wrong that could cause pain or sorrow. There is nothing in the kingdom of God that can cause discomfort, pain, suffering, or anxiety in even the smallest way.

The kingdom we are living in now (the church), and the kingdom we shall someday enter when we leave this world is called the kingdom of heaven, or the kingdom of God, and both of them are one and the same kingdom. Mark wrote, "Now after John was delivered up, Jesus came into Galilee, preaching the gospel of God, and saying, The time is fulfilled, and the kingdom of God is at hand: repent ye, and believe in the gospel" (Mark 1:14-15). Matthew wrote, "And as ye go, preach, saying, The kingdom of heaven is at hand" (Matthew 10:7). The kingdom of heaven came to earth on the Day of Pentecost, and that is the day the church was established.

When Jesus comes again and this world is consumed by fervent fire and dissolved, and the new heaven and the new earth are established, the church, the kingdom of God, and the kingdom of heaven will all be called the new heaven and the new earth. Peter wrote,

> Knowing this first, that in the last days mockers shall come with mockery, walking after their own lusts, and saying, Where is the promise of his coming? for, from the day that the fathers fell asleep,

all things continue as they were from the beginning of the creation. For this they willfully forget, that there were heavens from of old, and an earth compacted out of water and amidst water, by the word of God; by which means the world that then was, being overflowed with water, perished: but the heavens that now are, and the earth, by the same word have been stored up for fire, being reserved against the day of judgment and destruction of ungodly men. But forget not this one thing, beloved, that one day is with the Lord as a thousand years, and a thousand years as one day. The Lord is not slack concerning his promise, as some count slackness; but is longsuffering to you-ward, not wishing that any should perish, but that all should come to repentance. But the day of the Lord will come as a thief; in the which the heavens shall pass away with a great noise, and the elements shall be dissolved with fervent heat, and the earth and the works that are therein shall be burned up. Seeing that these things are thus all to be dissolved, what manner of persons ought ye to be in all holy living and godliness, looking for and earnestly desiring the coming of the day of God, by reason of which the heavens being on fire shall be dissolved, and the elements shall melt with fervent heat? But, according to his promise, we look for new heavens and a new earth, wherein dwelleth righteousness. Wherefore, beloved, seeing that ye look for these things, give diligence that ye may be found in peace, without spot and blameless in his sight. And account that the longsuffering of our Lord is

> salvation; even as our beloved brother Paul also, according to the wisdom given to him, wrote unto you. (2 Peter 3:3-15)

The kingdom of God is the place where righteousness lives, and therefore it is also a place where evil and corruption cannot exist.

When Christians leave this world and enter the kingdom of God in heaven, they enter a kingdom that belongs to them. Luke wrote, "Yet seek ye his kingdom, and these things shall be added unto you. Fear not, little flock; for it is your Father's good pleasure to give you the kingdom" (Luke 12:31-32). Christians have exactly what Adam had, and much more. Just as Adam was given the world that God created in six days, the original creation, and Adam was given complete control over that world (Genesis 1:26-27), so also the children of God are given the kingdom of God, and they have the authority to rule over that kingdom forever because it belongs to them. Luke wrote, "Yet seek ye his kingdom, and these things shall be added unto you. Fear not, little flock; for it is your Father's good pleasure to give you the kingdom" (Luke 12:31-32). The Hebrew writer said,

> For not unto angels did he subject the world to come, whereof we speak. But one hath somewhere testified, saying, What is man, that thou art mindful of him? Or the son of man, that thou visitest him? Thou madest him a little lower than the angels; Thou crownedst him with glory and honor, And didst set him over the works of thy hands: Thou didst put all things in subjection under his feet. For in that he subjected all things unto him, he left nothing that is not subject to him. But now we see not yet all things subjected to him. (Hebrews 2:5-8)

Jesus loves his children so much that he does not rule over them, he has made them to reign with him. Paul wrote, "Faithful is the saying: For if we died with him, we shall also live with him: if we endure, we shall also reign with him: if we shall deny him, he also will deny us" (2 Timothy 2:11-12). We sit in a very high place as we reign over God's kingdom with Jesus. Luke wrote, "But ye are they that have continued with me in my temptations; and I appoint unto you a kingdom, even as my Father appointed unto me, that ye may eat and drink at my table in my kingdom; and ye shall sit on thrones judging the twelve tribes of Israel" (Luke 22:28-30). For this reason we should not fear death, but look to it as the time when we shall leave sin, pain, suffering and death behind, and we shall enter a perfect world where righteousness, peace, glory, and life dominate forever.

John said that when a person enters the kingdom of heaven they shall see God *even as he is*, and they shall be like him. John wrote, "Beloved, now are we children of God, and it is not yet made manifest what we shall be. We know that, if he shall be manifested, we shall be like him; for we shall see him even as he is, and every one that hath this hope set on him purifieth himself, even as he is pure" (1 John 3:2-3). Matthew wrote, "Blessed are the pure in heart: for they shall see God" (Matthew 5:8). It is there we can shake the hand of Jesus and personally thank him for giving us a place to live with him in his kingdom forever—and it is the place where we can truly start making long range plans.

After Moses had served the Almighty for several years, he wanted to know who he was working for, and he asked God, "Show me, I pray thee, thy glory" (Exodus 33:18). God's reply was, "Thou canst not see my face; for man shall not see me and live" (Exodus 33:20). John said that Christians shall see God face to face, even as he is, and that they shall be like Him. What great changes Jesus made when he abolished sin and death and established righteousness and life!

There is a great advantage to those who believe in Jesus and that he has conquered death for all by his cross and resurrection. Many wives have lost their husbands to death, and husbands have lost their wives; and there are families that have lost brothers, children, and friends to death. There are many of our loved ones who have gone off to war and did not return. Those precious souls have not perished, they have gone on to their final home in heaven and we shall see them again. Death does not destroy our relationship with each other if we are in Christ; it might make a long-term separation, like sleep, but it is by no means final—we shall be with our loved ones again. That is something worth looking forward to.

Consider the extremely high place the children of God's occupy when they have been given life for one reason—the human family lives because God created it so that He might have children to love, and he wants his children to love him in return. He loved his children so very much that He gave them His own Spirit, the Holy Spirit (Hebrews 12:9) to give them life. Then he loved them so much, even after they turned to evil and sinned, that he came into the world as a man and died on a cross in their place so they might live. God is love, and such great love is infinite and far above understanding.

CHAPTER 1

The World God Created for Adam and His Children was Perfect and Beautiful

THE WORLD GOD CREATED for Adam and Eve was perfect—it held such excellence and perfection that it could not be improved upon in any way. During the six days of creation after a day's work God said, "*It is good!*" After the six days of the creation, on the final day when all was finished God said, "*It is very good!*" Moses wrote, "And God saw everything that he had made, and, behold, it was very good. And there was evening and there was morning, the sixth day" (Genesis 1:31).

God created the world so he would have something beautiful and of infinite value to give his children. God loved his children so very much that he gave them the world He created, and he gave them complete control of it (Genesis 1:26-29).

On the first day of creation God made the heavens (space, a place to put things); He made the earth (material, or mass—the original 118 elements, the objects to put in space); then He created light, the power to run the universe. The last thing God created was time, evening and morning, a way to establish the moment something had happened or when something was going to happen. I have often wondered why God said evening and morning—as we think it would be morning and evening. It is impossible to even imagine what was here before God created space. It seems the only thing that could have existed before God created the heavens and the earth was the eternal kingdom of God.

The first seven days of the creation are the beginning of history and the beginning of time, and those days were such days as we know today. "*Pre-historical*" does not exist for a person who has a Bible, for in that Book they have the history of the world from the beginning, the very first day, to the end, the very last day. When men try to substitute time for God to build a world, and time becomes the creator, it takes a tremendous amount of it because it is not possible to substitute God with time.

The four elements mentioned above: space, mass, energy, and time are the necessary elements for the universe to function—and it did not happen by evolution, or by chaos, for evolution, as Darwin viewed it, is chaos. The creation came into existence by the power of the Almighty and at the command of his Word. The theory of evolution has only one purpose, and that purpose is to destroy belief in the existence of God and establish men as the supreme power and the highest rulers over all things.

For the theory of evolution to achieve its purpose it must explain the origin of the creation and the beginning of life, but without considering the existence of the almighty God who is the One who accomplished that. The evolutionist believes the world did really not have a beginning; somehow, it has just always been here. They believe that something happened to that world that created life, like a lightning bolt striking water and creating a living cell, and that cell evolved into a man, and a woman; after that it took both the man and the women, with a special relationship between them, to procreate another human being, a little baby. Then there is another question: if that one living cell was the only living thing on earth, what did it feed on to survive and evolve? Evolution is a theory, it is chaos, it is void of reason, and it is impossible.

Mister Huxley was known as Darwin's bulldog, and he was as enthused about evolution as was Darwin. The one-hundredth anniversary of Darwin's book was celebrated in 1957 and Mister Huxley was the host. He started the meeting by telling his audience that they had come together to celebrate Darwin and the book he had written some one-hundred years ago: *The Theory of Evolution and Natural Selection*. He said, "We know that evolution is impossible, it just can't function—but it's all we have!" He refused to accept even the thought it was the Almighty who created the world and who is the Creator and the life-giver of all living creatures.

Moses' account of explaining the origin of the creation begins by describing each day in the same manner. Moses wrote six times for the six days, "And God said...and there was evening and morning, one day." Not only does the Bible declare it was God who spoke the world into existence, it states how long it took for Him do so (six days), and it declares what God did on each one of those days.

When God started his work on the first day of the creation (Sunday) it was morning, and on that morning God spoke what he had designed in his mind. The Psalmist wrote, "By the word of Jehovah were the heavens made, and all the host of them by the breath of his mouth" (Psalms 33:6). The Word physically created what the Father spoke; He created space, mass, light, and time. Then the Holy Spirit went to work to do His part, for the creation had no order, it was waste and void (Genesis 1:2). The Spirit moved, or *vibrated* over the world, and He created order. He established all the laws by which the world functions; He created the law of gravity, the law of energy (or thermodynamics), the law of motion (or inertia); He created all the natural laws by which the world functions, and those laws are the laws of God that cannot be broken—except by the Almighty himself if that becomes necessary. After God finished a day's work it was evening, the end of the day, and thus Moses wrote, "and there was evening and morning, one day."

Peter said the earth was formed by water (2 Peter 3:5) and after God formed it, it was completely immersed in water until the third day. It is difficult to understand how in the beginning of time the earth could be inundated with water and later something could happen that would cause dry land to appear and become the covering of a great part of the earth, as much as one-third of the surface of the globe. The Bible has the answer to that dilemma. Moses wrote,

> And God said, Let the waters under the heavens be gathered together unto one place, and let the dry land appear: and it was so. And God called the dry land Earth; and the gathering together of the waters called he Seas: and God saw that it was good. And God said, Let the earth put forth grass, herbs yielding seed, and fruit-trees bearing fruit after their kind, wherein is the seed thereof, upon the earth: and it was so. And the earth brought forth grass, herbs yielding seed after their kind, and trees bearing fruit, wherein is the seed thereof, after their kind: and God saw that it was good. And there was evening and there was morning, a third day. (Genesis 1:9–13)

When God created something with life, something living, he put a seed in it that would reproduce that organism exactly like it was when God made it, no more and no less. He said that all things shall reproduce, but "*after its kind,*" and God established the way that was achieved by what we call DNA, Deoxyribonucleic Acid. DNA was discovered in 1953 by James Watson and Francis Crick who received the Nobel Prize for their discovery and became famous for their work.

According to google, "DNA is the molecule that carries the genetic instructions for the development, functioning, growth, and reproduction of all known organisms, acting like a detailed blueprint for building and operating a living being, with its code stored in a twisting ladder-like structure called a double helix, made of four chemical bases to form the rungs." That complex "*ladder*" untwists in a flash, reproduces itself exactly, and then twists back together at the speed of light. God is amazing.

DNA cannot be changed or modified in any way. A gorilla has ninety-six percent of the DNA of a human (a banana has forty percent), but that four percent cannot be manipulated to make a human being out of a gorilla. Therefore, it did not happen all by itself over billions of years. The way God made things in the beginning are exactly the way they are today.

About 1,656 years after the creation the earth was once again immersed in water by the universal flood. It was the second day of creation that helps us understand where all of the water came from that caused the great flood, along with the fountains of the deep erupting. Moses wrote,

> And God said, Let there be a firmament in the midst of the waters, and let it divide the waters from the waters. And God made the firmament, and divided the waters which were under the firmament from the waters which were above the firmament: and it was so. And God called the firmament Heaven. And there was evening and there was morning, a second day. (Geneses 1:6-8)

It was the waters in the heavens that fell to the earth as rain, and with the rain and fountains of the deep breaking up the earth was quickly immersed in water. Moses wrote,

> And it came to pass after the seven days, that the waters of the flood were upon the earth. In the six hundredth year of Noah's life, in the second month, on the seventeenth day of the month, on the same day were all the fountains of the great deep broken up, and the windows of heaven were opened. And the rain was upon the earth forty days and forty nights. (Genesis 7:10–12)

There are men who have studied science who are in agreement with the Bible, that the earth has been completely immersed in water at least twice, for there are geologic formations that prove that to be a fact.

The second day of the creation can be a little difficult to understand; Moses wrote that the waters that covered the earth were separated from the waters that were above the earth, and the waters that were above the earth were even above the heavens.

The Jews believed there were three heavens; the first heaven was where there was air and it was where the birds flew. The second heaven was space where there were galaxies, stars, and planets. The third heaven, as Paul called it (2 Corinthians 12:2) is the spiritual home of God, and it is not physically connected to this world in any way.

Since the earth was covered with water, even above the highest mountains, there were immeasurable quantities of water covering the earth. The waters that were above the heavens were just as great as the waters that covered the earth. That means there was as much water above the world—and even above the heavens—as there was covering the earth. The water above the earth could not have been contained in clouds; no cloud could hold that much water. Also, at that early time it had never rained on the earth (Genesis 2:5), and so there were no clouds.

I have read the works of very intelligent scientists who are also Christians. Some of them are in the Christian Research Institute and they believe the Bible to be what it is—the Word of God. They are highly educated men who have PhD's in their fields of science, they believe that the world was formed in six days, and that they believe they were days such as we experience today, about twenty-four hour days. They also believe the earth to be about 6,000 years old. Christians can prove why they believe the world to be about 6,000 years old; just read Luke chapter 3; it contains the genealogy of Jesus from Adam to the Christ, and the men listed in that chapter from Adam to Christ did not live long enough to account for the earth being billions of years old, as the atheists believe.

Those men who have studied science and have put the Bible and science together believe the earth was formed by the Word of God, and it was changed into what it is today by forces so great they cannot be measured, such as the great flood, earthquakes, hurricanes—and not by gentle rains and winds over millions or billions of years as the evolutionist believes. I believe what these men have taught me by reading their words—because they have great educations in their fields of study—and because they are men of science as well as men of God. Their teachings are trustworthy because they believe the Bible to be the Word of God, and because they really make a lot of sense.

The men mentioned above believe that the water that was above the earth was in the form of a massive water-vapor shield that protected the earth from the direct radiation of the sun. That might be part of the answer as to why people lived so long up the time of Noah, over 900 years (Genesis 9:29). That water-vapor shield would have created an environment on earth such as a greenhouse would create resulting in moderate temperatures everywhere on earth, day and night, from the poles to the equator. Remember, when Adam and Eve were created, they never wore clothes, and they slept without clothes (Genesis 2:25). That would require a tropical climate.

If the water-vapor shield view is correct it would explain why the north and south poles were once tropical terrains, and why there were forests in Antarctica where dinosaurs once roamed. The fossils of dinosaurs and other tropical animals, and of tropical vegetation, have been found in the Antarctic. Those forests have turned into frozen fossilized coal beds buried in ice.

On the other hand, In the Artic region of Siberia, close to the North Pole, there are innumerable frozen fossils of mastodons, tropical animals, and tropical vegetation all buried in ice. The change in the weather was caused by the collapse of the water-vapor shield; when it broke it caused the forty-day rain that flooded the earth—along with the fountains of the deep breaking up—quite a reasonable conclusion.

The Bible says the rain lasted forty days and forty nights (Genesis 7:12), and the flood lasted about a year. When the water vapor broke it quickly flooded the entire world, and at the same time it immediately caused the earth to depend on direct radiation from the sun. Since there was practically no radiation from the sun whatsoever to warm the areas at the north and south poles those areas immediately became frozen wastelands of nothing but ice. It all happened so quickly that the mastodons that were living in present-day Siberia were flash-frozen while they still had green grass and flowers in their mouths and stomachs. They did not suffer; it happened so quickly that they never even felt the change in the weather.

Mastodons were tropical animals, and they depended on enormous amounts of vegetation for their survival. I have read in periodicals that when Siberian natives find a frozen mastodon they cut it up into pieces and feed the meat to their dogs. (Incidentally, scientists have said that there is more ivory in

Siberia than there is in both Africa and India combined). Is there a better explanation as to how the North Pole and South Pole were once tropical climates, and how they so very quickly became frozen wastelands?

After God had completed the last day of creation and he had exactly what he wanted, he said: "*It was very good.*" It was very good because it was perfect, and the entire creation was in harmony with God, with man, and with itself. Death and confusion did not exist because men and animals were vegetarians and no animals were slaughtered for food. Moses wrote,

> And God said, Behold, I have given you every herb yielding seed, which is upon the face of all the earth, and every tree, in which is the fruit of a tree yielding seed; to you it shall be for food: and to every beast of the earth, and to every bird of the heavens, and to everything that creepeth upon the earth, wherein there is life, I have given every green herb for food: and it was so. And God saw everything that he had made, and, behold, it was very good. And there was evening and there was morning, the sixth day. (Genesis 1:29-31).

The final day came after God completed his work and he had made a perfect and beautiful world; there was nothing in it that was unorganized, threatening, hurtful, or unpleasant. There was no sin, no law, and no death—with the exception of one simple commandment (or law) God gave Adam. Moses wrote, "And Jehovah God commanded the man, saying, Of every tree of the garden thou mayest freely eat: but of the tree of the knowledge of good and evil, thou shalt not eat of it: for in the day that thou eatest thereof thou shalt surely die" (Genesis 2:16-17). It is here we see the origin of law, sin, disobedience, death, and judgment.

Had sin not entered God's world it would have remained perfect and glorious forever, and there was only one law God had given to Adam that he could break and sin. But Adam and Eve broke that one law, and they sinned—and their transgression passed on to the entire creation and condemned everything God made (Romans 5:12; 8:20-22). However, God knows all things, and he knew that this was going to happen and He was prepared for it. God had a plan, and that plan was to restore the creation back into its original perfection by the death of his only begotten Son—on a cross; His name is Jesus, and such is the power of the cross, and the power of Jesus.

It is difficult to understand how any man could have such destructive power that he could commit a transgression that was so great it would not only condemn the man himself, but it would also condemn the entire creation and everyone and everything in it. But there was such a man, his name was Adam, and it was Adam who demonstrated the true destructive power of transgression. It is also impossible to understand, without revelation, how another man could have even greater power, infinite power, to undo the condemnation the first man caused and restore all things to their original beauty and perfection—and better. We know from experience that there are things that take years to build, such as the World Trade Centers, and we also know how they can be destroyed in a moment.

There was such a Man who had the power to abolish the consequences of Adam's transgression, and His name is Jesus. He had the power and the authority to redeem the creation Adam had defiled and establish a new world that was perfect; that new world could not be defiled in any way because it is forever protected by the blood of Jesus' cross. Jesus is also the Man who has the authority to forgive the man who caused the fall of the creation, and to forgive all sinners.

God's love for his children is the reason he created such a beautiful world to give them. What a horrible experience it was to so quickly lose it all just because of a horrible unpretentious act of disobedience.

God knew the problems and the difficulties he would have in building the creation, but He wanted something of unlimited value to give his children. God's world is an infinite universe that is filled with His glory; it is filled with galaxies and stars, with planets and moons beyond number, and with animals and trees that are indescribable, magnificent, and beyond measure. God also created many other things that were all made for the purpose of manifesting His infinite glory. Paul wrote, "For the invisible things of him since the creation of the world are clearly seen, being perceived through the things that are made, even his everlasting power and divinity; that they may be without excuse" (Romans 1:20). The world God made, the tangible and visible creation, is what we can see that declares the invisible qualities of its maker. God is Spirit and He cannot be seen, but His infinite glory and power can be perceived by what he made, and men who refuse to acknowledge that shall be held accountable.

Moses wrote, "And God made the two great lights; the greater light to rule the day, and the lesser light to rule the night: he made the stars also" (Genesis 1:16). After God used only five words to say it was He who made the stars he called them by their names. The Psalmist wrote, "He counteth the number of the stars; He calleth them all by their names" (Psalms 147:4). Men cannot begin to count the galaxies, let alone the infinite number of stars in just one of them! Take a good look at the Milky Way and you can see why. What a comfort it is to God's children for them to know that if God loves the stars so very much that he remembers each one of them by their name, then how much more does he love His beloved children who were all given life in His own image—and he knows his children by their names. Ezekiel wrote,

> Son of man, when a land sinneth against me by committing a trespass, and I stretch out my hand upon it, and break the staff of the bread thereof, and send famine upon it, and cut off from it man and beast; though these three men, Noah, Daniel, and Job, were in it, they should deliver but their own souls by their righteousness, saith the Lord Jehovah. (Ezekiel 14:13-14)

It is written in Jeremiah, "Then said Jehovah unto me, Though Moses and Samuel stood before me, yet my mind would not be toward this people: cast them out of my sight, and let them go forth" (Jeremiah 15:1). Moses wrote, "And Jehovah said unto Moses, I will do this thing also that thou hast spoken; for thou hast found favor in my sight, and I know thee by name" (Exodus 33:17). God knows his children by name, and some of them have accomplished such great works of faith that they have caused their Master to take notice, and they have etched a special place in His mind.

When we leave this world and enter the next we shall be the same person there we are here, but we will not be encumbered with a physical body. Apparently we shall have our same name, as did Job, Noah, and Moses.

When the spirit of a man leaves his the body, the body dies, and the spirit of the man returns to God to live in the new spiritual world. When the time comes that Jesus returns to this world and raises the dead, the day of the resurrection, all the bodies of the dead shall be raised and transformed into spiritual bodies. Even the bodies of little babies who died so young their bodies hadn't formed, such as babies that were aborted, shall be transformed and have a spiritual body.

Solomon was the wisest man who ever lived but he did not know what happened to the spirits of men, or beasts, when they left the body they had been dwelling in to keep it alive. It is written in First Kings 1:29-31,

> And God gave Solomon wisdom and understanding exceeding much, and largeness of heart, even as the sand that is on the sea-shore. And Solomon's wisdom excelled the wisdom of all the children of the east, and all the wisdom of Egypt. For he was wiser than all men; than Ethan the Ezrahite, and Heman, and Calcol, and Darda, the sons of Mahol: and his fame was in all the nations round about.

Solomon wrote, "Who knoweth the spirit of man, whether it goeth upward, and the spirit of the beast, whether it goeth downward to the earth?" (Ecclesiastes 3:21). We have learned a little more about death and where the spirits of men go when they die than what Solomon knew, and we have learned that by the teachings of Christ, and by his resurrection. We know the spirits of Just men made perfect by believing in Christ shall enter Paradise when they leave a person's body, and we know the spirits of unbelievers enter Hades (Luke 16:19-31).

It is interesting to learn that animals have spirits that give them life just as do men. We do not know any more about what happens to the spirit of an animal when it leaves the animal's body than Solomon knew. Is it possible they shall enter the new heaven and the new earth to be the animal friends of men there just as they are here? The bond between men and animals can become very strong, just as strong as is the bond between men. Paul wrote

> But some one will say, How are the dead raised? and with what manner of body do they come? Thou foolish one, that which thou thyself sowest is not quickened except it die: and that which

> thou sowest, thou sowest not the body that shall be, but a bare grain, it may chance of wheat, or of some other kind; but God giveth it a body even as it pleased him, and to each seed a body of its own. All flesh is not the same flesh: but there is one flesh of men, and another flesh of beasts, and another flesh of birds, and another of fishes. There are also celestial bodies, and bodies terrestrial: but the glory of the celestial is one, and the glory of the terrestrial is another. There is one glory of the sun, and another glory of the moon, and another glory of the stars; for one star differeth from another star in glory. So also is the resurrection of the dead. It is sown in corruption; it is raised in incorruption: it is sown in dishonor; it is raised in glory: it is sown in weakness; it is raised in power: it is sown a natural body; it is raised a spiritual body. If there is a natural body, there is also a spiritual body. So also it is written, the first man Adam became a living soul. The last Adam became a life-giving spirit. (1 Corinthians 15:35-45)

God is the Father of our spirits, and therefore spiritually we are just like our Father who is the Almighty—we are family. The Hebrew writer said "Furthermore, we had the fathers of our flesh to chasten us, and we gave them reverence: shall we not much rather be in subjection unto the Father of spirits, and live?" (Hebrews 12:9). We are more like God than we can imagine. When a person becomes a Christian and the blood of Jesus washes away all their sins they become a child of God, and at that very moment they become as righteous as God himself is righteous. John said, "My little children, let no man lead you astray: he that doeth righteousness is righteous, even as he is righteous" (1 John 3:7). Peter said when one is purified from sin by the blood of Jesus they become holy, and they are just as holy as God himself is holy. Peter said, "but like as he who called you is holy, be ye yourselves also holy in all manner of living; because it is written, Ye shall be holy; for I am holy" (1 Peter 1:15-16). What a wonderful life God has given his children to live and what a beautiful and glorious place He has given them to live in.

CHAPTER 2

When Adam Sinned He Condemned God's Perfect World and Sentenced It To Death

AFTER ADAM SINNED HE no longer owned the World God had given him, the world owned him and he became part of it. If one desires to view the power of sin and how destructive it can be, all they must do is consider the perfect world God gave Adam, how beautiful it was, and then consider how sin had conquered it and destroyed it. Also, one can view the standing men had with God when there was no sin and see how sin destroyed that relationship. Before sin Adam and Eve had a beautiful relationship with the Father as his children. They walked with Him and talked with Him just as good friends should and do (Genesis 3:8). After they sinned they were forced out the beautiful garden they once owned and enjoyed, and they were faced with living in an unfamiliar world they knew nothing about. Adam became subject to grievous labor and hard times. God explained to Adam what he was about to experience because of his sin, and it was not pleasant; it was horrifying. God said to Adam,

> Because thou hast hearkened unto the voice of thy wife, and hast eaten of the tree, of which I commanded thee, saying, Thou shalt not eat of it: cursed is the ground for thy sake; in toil shalt thou eat of it all the days of thy life; thorns also and thistles shall it bring forth to thee; and thou shalt eat the herb of the field; in the sweat of thy face shalt thou eat bread, till thou return unto the ground; for out of it wast thou taken: for dust thou art, and unto dust shalt thou return. And the man called his wife's name Eve; because she was the mother of all living. And Jehovah God made for Adam and for his wife coats of skins, and clothed them. And Jehovah God said, Behold, the man is become as one of us, to know good and evil; and now, lest he put forth his hand, and take also of the tree of life, and eat, and live for ever – therefore Jehovah God sent him forth from the garden of Eden, to till the ground from whence he was taken. So he drove out the man; and he placed at the east of the garden of Eden the Cherubim, and the flame of a sword which turned every way, to keep the way of the tree of life. (Genesis 3:17-24)

The very first animal sacrifice that was necessary was the animals that died at the hand of God so their skins could become the covering for His children. If Adam and Eve witnessed their bloody death and the cost of their covering, it would not be something they would soon forget. We know very little about what happened to Adam and Eve after they sinned, other than they were driven from their garden into a hard cruel world, and

Adam lived 930 years (Genesis 5:5). After Adam sinned men started following his example, and sin became so prevalent, so evil, and so powerful that God destroyed the entire world by a great flood. Moses wrote,

> And Jehovah saw that the wickedness of man was great in the earth, and that every imagination of the thoughts of his heart was only evil continually. And it repented Jehovah that he had made man on the earth, and it grieved him at his heart. And Jehovah said, I will destroy man whom I have created from the face of the ground; both man, and beast, and creeping things, and birds of the heavens; for it repenteth me that I have made them. But Noah found favor in the eyes of Jehovah. (Genesis 6:5-8)

We know the rest of the story; Noah was commanded to build an arc to save his family and the animal population. He was told that God would send him a male and a female animal of each species to repopulate the earth after the arc landed and the waters of the flood subsided.

It was some 1,656 years after the creation when the animals left the arc, and their world was not the same as it was before the flood; it was as different as night is from day. Men did not start eating animals, and animals did not start eating each other, until after the flood. That was the time when great animosity started to exist between men and beasts, between men and men, between nations and nations, and between the beasts themselves. Before Adam sinned he owned the world, it was his, and everything in it was subject to Adam's command. Moses wrote,

> And God said, Let us make man in our image, after our likeness: and let them have dominion over

> the fish of the sea, and over the birds of the heavens, and over the cattle, and over all the earth, and over every creeping thing that creepeth upon the earth. And God created man in his own image, in the image of God created he him; male and female created he them. (Genesis 1:26-27)

But Adam sinned, and his transgression caused him to lose it all. After his sin the world owned him, and he lost control of everything. He was subject to unpleasant task work throughout all of the unpleasant and uncertain days he was left to live. God told Adam,

And the fear of you and the dread of you shall be upon every beast of the earth, and upon every bird of the heavens; with all wherewith the ground teemeth, and all the fishes of the sea, into your hand are they delivered. Every moving thing that liveth shall be food for you; as the green herb have I given you all. But flesh with the life thereof, which is the blood thereof, shall ye not eat. (Genesis 9:2-4)

There were no food laws up to and during the time of Noah; food laws were established when Moses was given the Law of God on the Mount, and those food laws were only for the chosen people of God, for Zion, or the nation of Israel. The Psalmist wrote,

> Praise Jehovah, O Jerusalem; Praise thy God, O Zion. For he hath strengthened the bars of thy gates; He hath blessed thy children within thee. He maketh peace in thy borders; He filleth thee with the finest of the wheat. He sendeth out his commandment upon earth; His word runneth very swiftly. He giveth snow like wool; He scattereth the hoar-frost like ashes. He casteth forth his ice like morsels: Who can stand before his

> cold? He sendeth out his word, and melteth them: He causeth his wind to blow, and the waters flow. He hath not dealt so with any nation; And as for his ordinances, they have not known them. Praise ye Jehovah. (Psalms 147:12-20)

There was one food law that was given when the children of God left the arc; it was the forbidding of eating blood. The life of an animal is in its blood, and that life belongs to God; therefore it is holy. Blood cannot be used for common purposes such as food; it can only be used in sacrificial services as God commands. The spirit and the blood must be closely united because Moses said, "the life of the flesh is in the blood" (Leviticus 16:11), and Jesus said "the flesh profits nothing, it is the spirit that gives life" (John 6:63). Life is not common, it is holy. The law forbidding the eating of blood existed for all people from the day the children of God left the arc and started eating the flesh of animals up to and during the time of Moses, and it is still in force to this day. Moses wrote:

> And whatsoever man there be of the house of Israel, or of the strangers that sojourn among them, that eateth any manner of blood, I will set my face against that soul that eateth blood, and will cut him off from among his people. For the life of the flesh is in the blood; and I have given it to you upon the altar to make atonement for your souls: for it is the blood that maketh atonement by reason of the life. Therefore I said unto the children of Israel, No soul of you shall eat blood, neither shall any stranger that sojourneth among you eat blood. And whatsoever man there be of the children of Israel, or of the strangers that sojourn among them, who taketh in hunting

> any beast or bird that may be eaten; he shall pour out the blood thereof, and cover it with dust. For as to the life of all flesh, the blood thereof is all one with the life thereof: therefore I said unto the children of Israel, Ye shall eat the blood of no manner of flesh; for the life of all flesh is the blood thereof: whosoever eateth it shall be cut off. (Leviticus 17:10-14)

The law forbidding the eating blood is in force today, and it will be forever. Paul was on his first missionary journey to establish churches throughout Asia, and he and Barnabas went to Antioch, and they found certain disciples there who had been taught by the Jews that they had to be circumcised and keep the law of Moses or they could not become Christians (Acts 15:1). This false doctrine caused great confusion amongst the brethren, and it initiated a problem that must be corrected, or Christianity could not survive. Paul, Barnabas, and others went to Jerusalem to speak with the apostles and the elders about this problem. There, in Jerusalem, all the holy men of God were in agreement that such teaching was not true and it could not be tolerated. Here is their conclusion: and this is the message Paul took to the saints in Antioch.

> That the residue of men may seek after the Lord, And all the Gentiles, upon whom my name is called, Saith the Lord, who maketh these things known from of old. Therefore my judgment is, that we trouble not them that from among the Gentiles turn to God; but that we write unto them, that they abstain from the pollutions of idols, and from fornication, and from what is strangled, and from blood...For Moses from generations of old hath in every city them that preach him,

> being read in the synagogues every sabbath. For it seemed good to the Holy Spirit, and to us, to lay upon you no greater burden than these necessary things: that ye abstain from things sacrificed to idols, and from blood, and from things strangled, and from fornication; from which if ye keep yourselves, it shall be well with you. Fare ye well. So they, when they were dismissed, came down to Antioch; and having gathered the multitude together, they delivered the epistle. And when they had read it, they rejoiced for the consolation. (Acts 15:17-21, 28-31)

If the Gentiles who became Christians long after the day of Pentecost were taught something by the apostles as doctrine, then what they were taught would remain in effect for all Christians until the Lord comes again. They were taught that there shall be no idolatry (the worshipping of idols); there shall be no adultery or fornication, there shall be no eating blood, and there shall be no eating anything that had been strangled and the blood had not been drained from the body. If the church was taught in the second century that adultery and fornication were wrong, and if it is still wrong today, then so is the eating of blood wrong. The reason it is wrong to eat blood is because the life of an animal is in its blood, and that life is holy, it belongs to God.

Had there been no sin there would have been no law regarding the use or purpose of blood; but when men sinned, beginning with Adam, the sinner was sentenced to death. However, for most sins committed under the Old Covenant the sinner could offer the blood of an animal as a sacrifice so the animal could die in their place and bear the burden and guilt of their sin, and the sinner could live. However, there were some sins under the Old Covenant that were unforgivable. Moses wrote,

> Ye shall have one law for him that doeth aught unwittingly, for him that is home-born among the children of Israel, and for the stranger that sojourneth among them. But the soul that doeth aught with a high hand, whether he be home-born or a sojourner, the same blasphemeth Jehovah; and that soul shall be cut off from among his people. Because he hath despised the word of Jehovah, and hath broken his commandment, that soul shall utterly be cut off; his iniquity shall be upon him. (Numbers 15:29-31)

Isaiah wrote, "And Jehovah of hosts revealed himself in mine ears, Surely this iniquity shall not be forgiven you till ye die, saith the Lord, Jehovah of hosts" (Isaiah 22:14). There were some transgressions that were so severe that no sacrifice could be offered to forgive them. Therefore, to see the horrible result and consequence of sin we must consider all the men who died because of sin, all the animals that were sacrificed because of sin, and all the blood of those animals that was required to take the sins away. Then we must consider the supreme sacrifice of infinite value, the very blood of the precious Son of God, the onetime sacrifice for all time, and for all sin, that truly took away all the sins of the world and washed them away. John wrote, "On the morrow he seeth Jesus coming unto him, and saith, Behold, the Lamb of God, that taketh away the sin of the world!" (John 1:29). The Hebrew writer said, "...who needeth not daily, like those high priests, to offer up sacrifices, first for his own sins, and then for the sins of the people: for this he did once for all, when he offered up himself" (Hebrew 7:27). Ananias said to Saul, who became Paul the apostle, "And now why tarriest thou? Arise, and be baptized, and wash away thy sins, calling on his name" (Acts 22:16). If there had been no sin the world would have remained beautiful and perfect just as it was when God created it and gave it to Adam. But sin permanently changed all of that. In many cities where there is a large population the streets are contaminated with filth from careless people who could not care less about sanitation, cleanliness and order. That all happened because of sin. Sin has also caused great disrespect between people when there are some who live only for their own gain and pleasure, and they could not care less who they hurt or what they must do to achieve that.

What a hope Christians have when they look forward to a new world that is beautiful and perfect, and where none of the above even exists. In that new word there is not the least little thing that is abhorrent, unpleasant, or out of place. In that new world there is great love one for all and all for one, and respect, admiration, kindness, and love is the way of life in that world. Paul called the life we shall have in that new world *life indeed* (1 Timothy 6:19) which means it is real life, genuine life, and perfect life just as it was when God created the world. Jesus called it *life abundantly* (John 10:10) which means there is more life than what is necessary.

For God to destroy sin and its consequences he must have something more powerful than sin to accomplish that, for sin is a force that is so powerful, and so wicked and destructive, that it can devastate and destroy an entire world—and that is exactly what Adam's sin did (Romans 8:20-22). The only power Satan has to cause people to sin is temptation, and he uses that power to corrupt and destroy all that God loves. But God has the power to overcome and destroy Satan and his works, and more; it is called "*THE CROSS*!" God must also have someone more powerful than Satan to destroy Satan with his works, and he does; His name is Jesus. The power of Jesus is in his blood, and it has the force necessary to kill Satan, to sentence him to the pit of the abyss forever (2 Peter 2:4), and to abolish all his evil works that have contaminated the world. Jesus' blood has the worth and the power to abolish death and pay in full for all the damage sin has caused. What a Man, what a Savior, and what a powerful and loving God Jesus is to be able to accomplish all of that.

For God to send someone into the world to redeem it from sin and death the one he sends must be of the highest quality, of the highest value, and of the highest caliber of any living being. He must have such worth that he is of more value than the entire creation; for if he is to redeem and restore the world from its fall, he must have something of more value than the creation to achieve that. The One who came and had that value was Jesus, for he is the Son of the great King. If a King was in trouble and his realm was in danger, and his son was in dire straits also; and the king must decide whether to save his empire or his son, it seems the king's choice would be obvious—He would save his Son. But that is not what our almighty King did: He gave his Son to die on the torture stake, on the cross, to save the creation from its fall.

The next chapter will view the value of the one who came to save the world from sin and death; in few words—He was the Word, the Almighty himself who was made flesh. It will also view what the One who came must do to prepare himself for the task ahead of him. It will view the life he lived and what he did throughout his life to prepare himself to become worthy of being the one who could offer a sacrifice of such great value that it would restore an entire fallen world from annihilation into the perfect and beautiful holy city of God. Such a task seems impossible, but with God, all things are possible.

CHAPTER 3

The Son of God is the One Who Came to Abolish Death, Destroy the Power of Satan, and Restore the Creation to Its Original Glory and Greater

For God to leave his Holy Place in heaven where He and his holiness were constantly protected by his mighty angels and his inapproachable light (1 Timothy 6:13–16)—and became a man— was initiated by a matter that was so severe it is beyond human comprehension, and it was caused by sin! One day Adam and Eve were standing by the forbidden tree and they were just looking at it, probably wondering—WHY? Satan's reply was, Why not? Satan, in the form of a serpent tempted Eve to eat of the tree's fruit; she was deceived, she ate, and she sinned. Adam was standing right there by her all of that time, and not being deceived but knowing full well what he was doing he ate, and he sinned. Moses wrote,

> Now the serpent was more subtle than any beast of the field which Jehovah God had made. And he said unto the woman, Yea, hath God said, Ye shall not eat of any tree of the garden? And the woman said unto the serpent, Of the fruit of the trees of the garden we may eat: but of the fruit of the tree which is in the midst of the garden, God hath said, Ye shall not eat of it, neither shall ye touch it, lest ye die. And the serpent said unto the woman, Ye shall not surely die: for God doth know that in the day ye eat thereof, then your eyes shall be opened, and ye shall be as God, knowing good and evil. And when the woman saw that the tree was good for food, and that it was a delight to the eyes, and that the tree was to be desired to make one wise, she took of the fruit thereof, and did eat; and she gave also unto her husband with her, and he did eat. And the eyes of them both were opened, and they knew that they were naked; and they sewed fig-leaves together, and made themselves aprons. (Genesis 3:1-7)

Adam was not deceived when he ate. Paul wrote, "For Adam was first formed, then Eve; and Adam was not beguiled, but the woman being beguiled hath fallen into transgression" (1 Timothy 2:13-14). It is useless to even try to understand why Adam disobeyed the Almighty so knowingly and so arrogantly, but he did. Eve caused a problem for all women by her forbidden action; she limited the authority that women have in the home and in marriage. Paul wrote,

> Let a woman learn in quietness with all subjection. But I permit not a woman to teach, nor to have dominion over a man, but to be in quietness. For Adam was first formed, then Eve; and Adam was not beguiled, but the woman being beguiled hath fallen into transgression: but she shall be saved through her child-bearing, if they continue in faith and love and sanctification with sobriety. (1Timothy 2:11–15)

> Wives, be in subjection unto your own husbands, as unto the Lord. For the husband is the head of the wife, as Christ also is the head of the church, being himself the saviour of the body. But as the church is subject to Christ, so let the wives also be to their husbands in everything. Husbands, love your wives, even as Christ also loved the church, and gave himself up for it; that he might sanctify it, having cleansed it by the washing of water with the word, that he might present the church to himself a glorious church, not having spot or wrinkle or any such thing; but that it should be holy and without blemish. (Ephesians 5:22-27)

Adam's sin condemned himself, the creation, and the human family. Paul wrote, "Therefore, as through one man sin entered into the world, and death through sin; and so death passed unto all men, for that all sinned" (Romans 5:12); "For as through the one man's disobedience the many were made sinners, even so through the obedience of the one shall the many be made righteous" (Romans 5:19). Adam's sin also condemned the creation and sentenced it to death (Romans 8:20–23).

God knew that was going to happen and he was prepared to take the necessary measures to annul the condemnation Adam's sin caused. God had established a plan in his mind before the foundation of the world that would annul Satan's power and terminate his evil deeds. God was not about to allow Satan to have his victory by destroying the creation and the entire human family with it, and even achieve that victory by forcing the Almighty to keep his own law that would require Him to punish sin and the sinner by the death penalty he had decreed against sin. Instead, by the Almighty's love, grace, and mercy He would offer the sacrifice Himself that would forgive Adam and Eve and restore the world back into its original perfection, and greater. God would achieve that by the blood of His only begotten Son, and the Almighty knew that when he created the world his Son would have to die on a cross to save it, and He knew that before the foundation of the world. Peter wrote,

> And if ye call on him as Father, who without respect of persons judgeth according to each man's work, pass the time of your sojourning in fear: knowing that ye were redeemed, not with corruptible things, with silver or gold, from your vain manner of life handed down from your fathers; but with precious blood, as of a lamb without spot, even the blood of Christ: who was foreknown indeed before the foundation of the world, but was manifested at the end of times for your sake, who through him are believers in God, that raised him from the dead, and gave him glory; so that your faith and hope might be in God. (1 Peter 1:17-21)

It is interesting to know that before sin came into the world, and even before the foundation of the world, all sins were forgiven before they were even committed. Mathew wrote,

> But when the Son of man shall come in his glory, and all the angels with him, then shall he sit on the throne of his glory: and before him shall be gathered all the nations: and he shall separate them one from another, as the shepherd separateth the sheep from the goats; and he shall set the sheep on his right hand, but the goats on the left. Then shall the King say unto them on his right hand, Come, ye blessed of my Father, inherit the kingdom prepared for you from the foundation of the world. (Matthew 25:31-34)

Paul wrote,

> Blessed be the God and Father of our Lord Jesus Christ, who hath blessed us with every spiritual blessing in the heavenly places in Christ: even as he chose us in him before the foundation of the world, that we should be holy and without blemish before him in love: having foreordained us unto adoption as sons through Jesus Christ unto himself, according to the good pleasure of his will, to the praise of the glory of his grace, which he freely bestowed on us in the Beloved: in whom we have our redemption through his blood, the forgiveness of our trespasses, according to the riches of his grace. (Ephesians 1:3-7)

For God to accomplish what he knew he must do to redeem his world, He knew that he must leave his throne of glory in heaven and become a man like other men. The writer of the Hebrew letter said,

> For it became him, for whom are all things, and through whom are all things, in bringing many sons unto glory, to make the author of their salvation perfect through sufferings. For both he that sanctifieth and they that are sanctified are all of one: for which cause he is not ashamed to call them brethren, saying, I will declare thy name unto my brethren, In the midst of the congregation will I sing thy praise. And again, I will put my trust in him. And again, Behold, I and the children whom God hath given me. Since then the children are sharers in flesh and blood, he also himself in like manner partook of the same; that through death he might bring to nought him that had the power of death, that is, the devil; and might deliver all them who through fear of death were all their lifetime subject to bondage. For verily not to angels doth he give help, but he giveth help to the seed of Abraham. (Hebrews 2:10-16)

For Christ to qualify himself to become the Sacrifice that would take away the sins of the world he must become a man; He must be born as all other babies are born, except He was born to a virgin. Then he must live on the earth exactly as other men live. He must face all of the temptations, dangers, snares, threats, and limitations that other men experience with no advantages over other men whatsoever to overcome them. He did that, the Hebrew writer said,

> Having then a great high priest, who hath passed through the heavens, Jesus the Son of God, let us hold fast our confession. For we have not a high priest that cannot be touched with the feeling of our infirmities; but one that hath been in all

> points tempted like as we are, yet without sin. (Hebrews 4:14-15)

At the end of his life he must offer His sinless life to God as a human sacrifice that would take away the sins of the world (John 1:29), pay in full for the damage sin had caused, and correct all of the problems sin had instigated. Jesus knew the task He faced before the foundation of the world. Paul wrote,

> And to make all men see what is the dispensation of the mystery which for ages hath been hid in God who created all things; to the intent that now unto the principalities and the powers in the heavenly places might be made known through the church the manifold wisdom of God, according to the eternal purpose which he purposed in Christ Jesus our Lord: in whom we have boldness and access in confidence through our faith in him. (Ephesians 3:9–12)

The Son of God came into the world to be called the Lamb of God (John 1:29), and His mission was to offer himself as a Sacrifice on a cross that would redeem the creation by cleansing it with his blood. The task that Jesus was sent to achieve was so great and so vital that God did not care enough to send the very best; he cared so much that he came himself. John wrote,

> In the beginning was the Word, and the Word was with God, and the Word was God. The same was in the beginning with God. All things were made through him; and without him was not anything made that hath been made. In him was life; and the life was the light of men. And the light shineth in the darkness; and the darkness

> apprehended it not...And the Word became flesh, and dwelt among us (and we beheld his glory, glory as of the only begotten from the Father), full of grace and truth. (John 1:1–5, 14)

The Redeemer whom God sent to save the world was the Word, almighty Jehovah God himself, the very one who created the heavens and the earth; and he had to become a man to achieve that. Jeremiah wrote,

> Behold, the days come, saith Jehovah, that I will raise unto David a righteous Branch, and he shall reign as king and deal wisely, and shall execute justice and righteousness in the land. In his days Judah shall be saved, and Israel shall dwell safely; and this is his name whereby he shall be called: Jehovah our righteousness. (Jeremiah 23:-5-6)

Jesus was the righteous Branch that Jehovah raised up, he was the Son of David (Matthew 1:1), and his name was *Jehovah our righteousness.* Isaiah wrote,

> For unto us a child is born, unto us a son is given; and the government shall be upon his shoulder: and his name shall be called Wonderful, Counsellor, Mighty God, Everlasting Father, Prince of Peace. Of the increase of his government and of peace there shall be no end, upon the throne of David, and upon his kingdom, to establish it, and to uphold it with justice and with righteousness from henceforth even for ever. The zeal of Jehovah of hosts will perform this. (Isaiah 9:6-7).

It is interesting that the Son who was born to the virgin Mary would be called Mighty God and Everlasting Father (the Son also being the eternal Father); but that was what He was called because that is who He was. It was the Father who lived in the Son who died on the cross for our sins! What would Mary have thought if when she was pregnant she knew she was carrying *Mighty God* and *Everlasting Father* in her womb?

What a day in heaven that must have been!—the very day the Word was to become flesh. We cannot begin to imagine what went on in heaven on that day when the Father, the Word, and the Holy Spirit were discussing the moment that had arrived, just as in the beginning when the Three of them deliberated how they would create a man in Their own image (Genesis 1:26). It was the moment when God's plan to redeem the world through the blood of his own Son must begin. It was the first time, and the only time that a member of the Godhead was to leave heaven and become something God had never been before—a man. The Father, by the workings of the Holy Spirit, was about to place a little seed in the womb of a virgin who was called Mary, and she was going to have His child, the Son of God. What went on in God's mind as he was about to send the Holy Spirit to place the seed that contained the Creator of the universe in Mary's womb? Jesus was born to a woman whose name was Mary and she was a virgin, and if anyone knew most certainly that Jesus was the Son of God, it was Mary.

One day an angel appeared to Mary and told her she was going to have a Son, and Mary knew that virgins do not have children. Luke wrote, "And Mary said unto the angel, How shall this be, seeing I know not a man?" (Luke 1:34). When Mary told her husband that she was pregnant, and how it happened, for some reason he would not believe her; he doubted her so seriously he was going to put her away. Matthew wrote,

> Now the birth of Jesus Christ was on this wise: When his mother Mary had been betrothed to Joseph, before they came together she was found with child of the Holy Spirit. And Joseph her husband, being a righteous man, and not willing to make her a public example, was minded to put her away privily. But when he thought on these things, behold, an angel of the Lord appeared unto him in a dream, saying, Joseph, thou son of David, fear not to take unto thee Mary thy wife: for that which is conceived in her is of the Holy Spirit. And she shall bring forth a son; and thou shalt call his name JESUS; for it is he that shall save his people from their sins. Now all this is come to pass, that it might be fulfilled which was spoken by the Lord through the prophet, saying, Behold, the virgin shall be with child, and shall bring forth a son, And they shall call his name Immanuel; which is, being interpreted, God with us. And Joseph arose from his sleep, and did as the angel of the Lord commanded him, and took unto him his wife; and knew her not till she had brought forth a son: and he called his name JESUS. (Matthew 1:18-25).

It took the Holy Spirit to convince Joseph that Mary was telling the truth, and what a relief that must have been to Joseph. Joseph loved Mary so dearly he would have died for her before he would have put her away, and for him to even think she had been unfaithful to him was blow he could not bear.

When Gabriel, the arc angel told Mary she was going to have a son, she questioned him, and there was no problem, she just did not understand. But when an angel appeared to Zacharias, who was a very old man, and told him that his wife, who was very old, was going to have a son, he did not believe such was possible. He asked the angel how such could be possible when he and his wife were very old and many years past being able to give birth to children. The angel's name was Gabriel, and he was not pleased with Zacharias' response, that any man would question the word of an angel. Zacharias was going to suffer for his disbelief. Luke wrote in his gospel,

> And Zacharias said unto the angel, Whereby shall I know this? for I am an old man, and my wife well stricken in years. And the angel answering said unto him, I am Gabriel, that stand in the presence of God; and I was sent to speak unto thee, and to bring thee these good tidings. And behold, thou shalt be silent and not able to speak, until the day that these things shall come to pass, because thou believedst not my words, which shall be fulfilled in their season. And the people were waiting for Zacharias, and they marvelled while he tarried in the temple. And when he came out, he could not speak unto them: and they perceived that he had seen a vision in the temple: and he continued making signs unto them, and remained dumb. (Luke 1:18-22)

Joseph and Mary were both moral and righteous people—and they were very poor, exactly the kind of couple the Almighty would choose to bear his Son. Just before Jesus was born they were traveling to Bethlehem, the town where they were required to enroll for the census and pay their taxes (Luke 2:1–7). They had gone to an inn for a place to spend the night, but there was no room for them in the inn, probably because they had very little money and who they were—peasants. So, instead of being escorted to a room they were directed to the animal stable, a place that was quite primitive and unsanitary—but it was the best that

Joseph and Mary could provide for the birth of God's Son. After Jesus was born he was wrapped in swaddling clothes and laid in a manger. A manger was an animal feeding trough. Why would Jesus' Father in heaven choose such horrible conditions for his own Son to be born? Maybe it was because his birth typified his entire life, for Jesus always lived just a few steps below abject poverty.

As Jesus grew he was taught by his earthly parents and by his heavenly Father. Is it possible to even imagine how Joseph felt teaching his Son, the creator of the world and builder of all things, how to saw a piece of wood and how to hold a hammer? Luke wrote in his gospel, "And the child grew, and waxed strong, filled with wisdom: and the grace of God was upon him...And Jesus advanced in wisdom and stature, and in favor with God and men" (Luke 2:40, 52).

Jesus was the Creator and the owner of the world He made, but when He lived in his own world he lived in poverty. There was an occasion when Jesus and Peter were going into the temple; there was a temple tax which was hardly anything at all, maybe about a penny, but it was more than Jesus and Peter had between them. The gospel of Matthew has the account.

> And when they were come to Capernaum, they that received the half-shekel came to Peter, and said, Doth not your teacher pay the half-shekel? He saith, Yea. And when he came into the house, Jesus spoke first to him, saying, What thinkest thou, Simon? the kings of the earth, from whom do they receive toll or tribute? from their sons, or from strangers? And when he said, From strangers, Jesus said unto him, Therefore the sons are free. But, lest we cause them to stumble, go thou to the sea, and cast a hook, and take up the fish that first cometh up; and when thou hast opened

> his mouth, thou shalt find a shekel: that take, and give unto them for me and thee. (Matthew 17:24–27)

It appears that Jesus never worried much about money. He never had a dime or a peso in his pocket, if he had a pocket, and he never owned anything throughout his entire life but the clothes he wore. The soldiers that crucified him took those (Matthew 27:35). John wrote,

> The soldiers therefore, when they had crucified Jesus, took his garments and made four parts, to every soldier a part; and also the coat: now the coat was without seam, woven from the top throughout. They said therefore one to another, Let us not rend it, but cast lots for it, whose it shall be: that the scripture might be fulfilled, which saith, They parted my garments among them, And upon my vesture did they cast lots. These things therefore the soldiers did. But there were standing by the cross of Jesus his mother, and his mother's sister, Mary the wife of Clopas, and Mary Magdalene. (John 19:23-35)

The scripture that was fulfilled was Psalms 22:17-18, "I may count all my bones; They look and stare upon me. They part my garments among them, and upon my vesture do they cast lots." It seems strange that such a trivial thing as parting Jesus' clothing amongst the soldiers when he died would be mentioned; however it was not trivial! It declares so certainly that the Psalmist knew so clearly exactly what would happen when Jesus was crucified that he could predict even the smallest details perfectly several hundred years before they occurred. How did Mary feel when she witnessed the soldiers casting lots for a garment she had so carefully made to give to her Son?

Throughout Jesus' life He did not even have a place to sleep. Matthew wrote, "And there came a scribe, and said unto him, Teacher, I will follow thee whithersoever thou goest. And Jesus saith unto him, The foxes have holes, and the birds of the heaven have nests; but the Son of man hath not where to lay his head" (Matthew 8:19–20). There was no response from the scribe. Evidently, Jesus lived like a street person lived—a person with no real home. But Jesus' real home was not in this world—His real home was a kingdom, and He was the King. It is called the Kingdom of heaven and the Kingdom of God, and Jesus was the King; He is the King of kings and the Lord of lords. Paul wrote,

> I charge thee in the sight of God, who giveth life to all things, and of Christ Jesus, who before Pontius Pilate witnessed the good confession; that thou keep the commandment, without spot, without reproach, until the appearing of our Lord Jesus Christ: which in its own times he shall show, who is the blessed and only Potentate, the King of kings, and Lord of lords; who only hath immortality, dwelling in light unapproachable; whom no man hath seen, nor can see: to whom be honor and power eternal. Amen. (1 Timothy 6:13-16)

Jesus gave up his equality with God and being the King of kings and the Lord of lords to become a man, and to become a human being like other men. Paul wrote,

> Have this mind in you, which was also in Christ Jesus: who, existing in the form of God, counted not the being on an equality with God a thing to be grasped, but emptied himself, taking the form

> of a servant, being made in the likeness of men; and being found in fashion as a man, he humbled himself, becoming obedient even unto death, yea, the death of the cross. Wherefore also God highly exalted him, and gave unto him the name which is above every name; that in the name of Jesus every knee should bow, of things in heaven and things on earth and things under the earth, and that every tongue should confess that Jesus Christ is Lord, to the glory of God the Father. (Philippians 2:5-11)

What a price the Word must pay to redeem a world that belonged to Him.

Since Jesus was a man like other men He experienced the same problems that other men faced. He was tempted in all points as other men are tempted, yet without sin (Hebrews 4:15). He knew hunger. Matthew wrote,

> Then was Jesus led up of the Spirit into the wilderness to be tempted of the devil. And when he had fasted forty days and forty nights, he afterward hungered. And the tempter came and said unto him, If thou art the Son of God, command that these stones become bread. But he answered and said, It is written, Man shall not live by bread alone, but by every word that proceedeth out of the mouth of God. (Matthew 4:1-4).

While Jesus was traveling with his disciples from Judea to Galilee there was a city he must pass through, even though it was out of his way. He went to that city to speak with a certain woman who wanted to be saved, but she knew not the way. When He entered the city He was very tired and thirsty and He sat down by the edge of a well while His disciples went into the village to purchase food. A Samaritan woman came to the well to draw water. She ignored Jesus, and so to get a drink of water and break the ice He asked her for a drink of her water. John wrote of this occurrence.

> And he must needs pass through Samaria. so he cometh to a city of Samaria, called Sychar, near to the parcel of ground that Jacob gave to his son Joseph: and Jacob's well was there. Jesus therefore, being wearied with his journey, sat thus by the well. It was about the sixth hour. There cometh a woman of Samaria to draw water: Jesus saith unto her, Give me to drink. For his disciples were gone away into the city to buy food. The Samaritan woman therefore saith unto him, How is it that thou, being a Jew, askest drink of me, who am a Samaritan woman? (For Jews have no dealings with Samaritans.) (John 4:4–9)

At that time it would have been very unusual for a man to speak to a woman; especially a Jewish man speaking to a Samaritan woman. But Jesus had ordered His journey to the place where He and his apostles were originally going so they must pass through Samaria, and he did that just so He could sit by that well and speak to that woman, for her soul was precious. Jesus accomplished the purpose of his communications with the Samaritan woman, because he converted her and the entire village from idolatry to Christianity. John wrote,

> And from that city many of the Samaritans believed on him because of the word of the woman, who testified, He told me all things that ever I did. So when the Samaritans came unto him, they

> besought him to abide with them: and he abode there two days. And many more believed because of his word; and they said to the woman, Now we believe, not because of thy speaking: for we have heard for ourselves, and know that this is indeed the Saviour of the world. (John 4:39-42)

After Jesus had lived to the age of about age 33 he had accomplished the purpose for which he came; He came to offer himself as a sacrifice that would take away the sins of the world, abolish death, and restore the creation into its formal glory as it was when God created it, and even greater. It is impossible to even imagine the power, the authority, and the strength it would take to abolish death, it seems impossible (2 Timothy 1:10). How could such a powerful force as death, an experience every living creature must suffer, suddenly just be abolished? But the power of the cross is greater than the power of law, sin and death, and it was by the way of the cross Jesus accomplished exactly what God sent him to do. God wanted his children to be set free from sin, death, and law, and He wanted them to have perfect freedom from all threatening forces. Paul wrote, "For freedom did Christ set us free: stand fast therefore, and be not entangled again in a yoke of bondage" (Galatians 5:1). God wanted His children to live in a perfect and beautiful world just as it was when he originally created it and gave it to Adam. Jesus promised all of his followers who believed in him that they would never die and they would never be judged, and such a promise is not easy to believe. John wrote,

> Verily, verily, I say unto you, He that heareth my word, and believeth him that sent me, hath eternal life, and cometh not into judgment, but hath passed out of death into life. (John 5:24).

> Verily, verily, I say unto you, If a man keep my word, he shall never see death. (John 8:51)

> Jesus said unto her, I am the resurrection, and the life: he that believeth on me, though he die, yet shall he live, and whosoever liveth and believeth on me shall never die. Believest thou this? (John 11:25–26)

> Your fathers ate the manna in the wilderness, and they died. This is the bread which cometh down out of heaven, that a man may eat thereof, and not die. I am the living bread which came down out of heaven: if any man eat of this bread, he shall live for ever: yea and the bread which I will give is my flesh, for the life of the world. (John 6:49–51)

When death entered the world because of sin it became the most feared event of all men. Job called it the king of terrors, "He shall be rooted out of his tent where he trusteth; And he shall be brought to the king of terrors" (Job 18:14). Why? It is because we know so very little about death. The fear of death is very great, not because of what we know about it, but because of what we do not know about it. We don't know when it will happen, but we know it will. The Hebrew writer said, "And inasmuch as it is appointed unto men once to die, and after this cometh judgment" (Hebrews 9:27).

There were several patients in a nursing home who were at the end of their lives and they had but a few days to live, and they knew that. They volunteered to be interviewed, and the purpose of the interview was to find out how they felt to be so close to death. Their response was not what the interviewers expected, they said they were not so much afraid of death, they knew it was coming, but they were extremely concerned about what happens after death.

Even as powerful and fearful death is, there are many who would lay down their life for another; for a dear friend or brother. In war, and at other times, that has happened. There are fathers and mothers who would not hesitate a moment to lay down their life to save their child. Even animals will give their lives to protect their siblings. But how many are there who would lay down the life of their child—the life of their son or their daughter—for any purpose, to save anyone or anything? But God did that very thing for us when he sent his Son into the world to lay down his life on the cross to save his children from law, sin, and death. John said, "For God so loved the world, that he gave his only begotten Son, that whosoever believeth on him should not perish, but have eternal life. For God sent not the Son into the world to judge the world; but that the world should be saved through him" (John 3:16-17).

What happens to a person then they die? The atheist believes they will just cease to exist in any form. Others believe they shall return to this world in another form—reincarnation. The believer who trusts in God believes they shall be carried away by the angels into God's new world, or Abraham's bosom; and it is written in the Bible of a man who had that experience. His name was Lazarus; not the Lazarus Jesus raised from the dead. He was a beggar who sat at a rich man's gate just wanting for something to eat, just the crumbs from his table. The rich man ignored him, as best he could, but there a came a day when they died. Luke wrote,

> Now there was a certain rich man, and he was clothed in purple and fine linen, faring sumptuously every day: and a certain beggar named Lazarus was laid at his gate, full of sores, and desiring to be fed with the crumbs that fell from

> the rich man's table; yea, even the dogs came and licked his sores. And it came to pass, that the beggar died, and that he was carried away by the angels into Abraham's bosom: and the rich man also died, and was buried. And in Hades he lifted up his eyes, being in torments, and seeth Abraham afar off, and Lazarus in his bosom. And he cried and said, Father Abraham, have mercy on me, and send Lazarus, that he may dip the tip of his finger in water, and cool my tongue; for I am in anguish in this flame. But Abraham said, Son, remember that thou in thy lifetime receivedst thy good things, and Lazarus in like manner evil things: but now here he is comforted, and thou art in anguish. And besides all this, between us and you there is a great gulf fixed, that they that would pass from hence to you may not be able, and that none may cross over from thence to us. And he said, I pray thee therefore, father, that thou wouldest send him to my father's house; for I have five brethren; that he may testify unto them, lest they also come into this place of torment. But Abraham saith, They have Moses and the prophets; let them hear them. And he said, Nay, father Abraham: but if one go to them from the dead, they will repent. And he said unto him, If they hear not Moses and the prophets, neither will they be persuaded, if one rise from the dead. (Luke 16:19-31)

Abraham's bosom, or Paradise, is the place the redeemed enter when their body dies and their spirit returns to God who gave it. Abraham's bosom is only mentioned once in the Bible, and Paradise is mentioned three times in the New Testament; it is the place the saints enter when they leave this world and enter the kingdom of God to have eternal fellowship with their Father. John wrote, "He that hath an ear, let him hear what the Spirit saith to the churches. To him that overcometh, to him will I give to eat of the tree of life, which is in the Paradise of God" (Revelation 2:7). Paradise is the word one would use to describe a beautiful walled garden.

When the time came that Jesus must face the cross and He must die, he gave himself up willingly to achieve that, for that is the reason he came. Throughout his ministry He tried to convince his disciples that the reason he was born was so he could die, and for a very special purpose. Luke wrote,

> And he took unto him the twelve, and said unto them, Behold, we go up to Jerusalem, and all the things that are written through the prophets shall be accomplished unto the Son of man. For he shall be delivered up unto the Gentiles, and shall be mocked, and shamefully treated, and spit upon: and they shall scourge and kill him: and the third day he shall rise again. And they understood none of these things; and this saying was hid from them, and they perceived not the things that were said. (Luke 18:31-34)

Many times Jesus tried to prepare his disciples for his departure, but they just could not understand what he was telling them. It was not because what Jesus said was complex and difficult to comprehend; it was because the message of his teaching was not possible for his disciples to believe to be true.

The time had come when Jesus must die, and he was with his disciples in the garden where he prayed. Judas was not with them, he was bargaining with the chief priests for thirty pieces of silver to take the police to Jesus' garden at a convenient time when his arrest would be easy and secure. Matthew wrote,

> Arise, let us be going: behold, he is at hand that betrayeth me. And while he yet spake, lo, Judas, one of the twelve, came, and with him a great multitude with swords and staves, from the chief priest and elders of the people. Now he that betrayed him gave them a sign, saying, Whomsoever I shall kiss, that is he: take him. And straightway he came to Jesus, and said, Hail, Rabbi; and kissed him. And Jesus said unto him, Friend, do that for which thou art come. Then they came and laid hands on Jesus, and took him. And behold, one of them that were with Jesus stretched out his hand, and drew his sword, and smote the servant of the high priest, and struck off his ear. Then saith Jesus unto him, Put up again thy sword into its place: for all they that take the sword shall perish with the sword. Or thinkest thou that I cannot beseech my Father, and he shall even now send me more than twelve legions of angels? How then should the scriptures be fulfilled that thus it must be? In that hour said Jesus to the multitudes, Are ye come out as against a robber with swords and staves to seize me? I sat daily in the temple teaching, and ye took me not. But all this is come to pass, that the scriptures of the prophets might be fulfilled. Then all the disciples left him, and fled. (Matthew 25:46-56)

Jesus was taken before the judges, not to have a real trial, but to be sentenced to death by crucifixion. There were two men with him facing the same punishment, and they were observing all the abuse Jesus was experiencing. Jesus received his sentence by a reluctant judge, Pilate, who knew Jesus was innocent. Matthew wrote,

> When therefore they were gathered together, Pilate said unto them, Whom will ye that I release unto you? Barabbas, or Jesus who is called Christ? For he knew that for envy they had delivered him up. And while he was sitting on the judgment-seat, his wife sent unto him, saying, Have thou nothing to do with that righteous man; for I have suffered many things this day in a dream because of him. Now the chief priests and the elders persuaded the multitudes that they should ask for Barabbas, and destroy Jesus. But the governor answered and said unto them, Which of the two will ye that I release unto you? And they said, Barabbas. Pilate saith unto them, What then shall I do unto Jesus who is called Christ? They all say, Let him be crucified. And he said, Why, what evil hath he done? But they cried out exceedingly, saying, Let him be crucified. So when Pilate saw that he prevailed nothing, but rather that a tumult was arising, he took water, and washed his hands before the multitude, saying, I am innocent of the blood of this righteous man; see ye to it. And all the people answered and said, His blood be on us, and on our children. Then released he unto them Barabbas; but Jesus he scourged and delivered to be crucified. (Matthew 27:17-26)

Jesus and the two malefactors were taken to Golgotha, the place of the skull where men were crucified. Jesus was crucified, and the two thieves were crucified with him. When He was in great pain and agony by being nailed to a cross, He was listening to all the insults and accusations that were being heaped upon him, and he said nothing; He just stayed calm. However, in just the short time that one of the malefactors had been with

Jesus during the time of his appearing before his judges, he understood who Jesus was and why he had come. He must have been a very intelligent and observing man. He had noticed the maltreatment Jesus had suffered, he heard all of the insults that had been heaped against him, and he himself had even joined in (Matthew 27:44). Then he observed how Jesus responded to such abuse—He just accepted it all and said nothing. Just before the three men died, with only minutes to live, one malefactor came to the firm conclusion that Jesus was being crucified for being exactly whom he claimed to be: He truly was the Son of God and the King of Israel, and he was here to establish a kingdom by his death. Luke wrote,

> And the people stood beholding. And the rulers also scoffed at him, saying, He saved others; let him save himself, if this is the Christ of God, his chosen. And the soldiers also mocked him, coming to him, offering him vinegar, and saying, If thou art the King of the Jews, save thyself. And there was also a superscription over him, THIS IS THE KING OF THE JEWS. And one of the malefactors that were hanged railed on him, saying, Art not thou the Christ? save thyself and us. But the other answered, and rebuking him said, Dost thou not even fear God, seeing thou art in the same condemnation? And we indeed justly; for we receive the due reward of our deeds: but this man hath done nothing amiss. And he said, Jesus, remember me when thou comest in thy kingdom. And he said unto him, Verily I say unto thee, Today shalt thou be with me in Paradise. (Luke 23:35–43

One of the thieves who were dying with Jesus looked to Him and asked him for forgiveness, and to remember Him when he came into his kingdom; Jesus forgave him and promised him he would be remembered. This illustrates one of the greatest examples of faith that can be found in the entire Bible, and one of the rarest and greatest cases of a soul being forgiven and brought to salvation. For here we view a dying man who was in great agony looking to another man who was dying with him, and asking that man to save him after they had both died. How did that man grasp all of that in just the few hours he had been with Jesus? That man had learned more about Jesus, who he was and why he came, than Peter and the rest of the apostles had learned in the three years they had been with him as his disciples.

What an example this is to all believers, especially to those who at times feel they are not worthy of being saved because of their many transgression, and because of how little they are able to accomplish for God. Everyone who feels that way should remember this incident and know that they have as much to offer God as that thief had to offer in just the few moments before he died. That man was saved by his faith, and that is the only way that anyone can be saved. Paul wrote,

> For by grace have ye been saved through faith; and that not of yourselves, it is the gift of God; not of works, that no man should glory. (Ephesians 2:8–9)

> Be not ashamed therefore of the testimony of our Lord, nor of me his prisoner: but suffer hardship with the gospel according to the power of God; who saved us, and called us with a holy calling, not according to our works, but according to his own purpose and grace, which was given us

> in Christ Jesus before times eternal. (2 Timothy 1:8-9)

> But when the kindness of God our Saviour, and his love toward man, appeared, not by works done in righteousness, which we did ourselves, but according to his mercy he saved us, through the washing of regeneration and renewing of the Holy Spirit, which he poured out upon us richly, through Jesus Christ our Saviour; that, being justified by his grace, we might be made heirs according to the hope of eternal life. (Titus 3:4–7)

The malefactor who died on the cross with Jesus and the poor man who sat at the rich man's gate begging for food went to Abraham's bosom or to Paradise when they died. The rich man, not because he was rich but because he was an unbeliever, went to Hades. There are some who believe that all souls enter Hades when the body dies, and that Hades is the place where all spirts go when they leave their body, and that is not so! Hades is the realm of dead spirits, not living spirits; Hades is the place of the lost! Hades is mentioned ten times in the New Testament, and in every case it is associated with punishment and death. Below is how Hades is described.

> And it came to pass, that the beggar died, and that he was carried away by the angels into Abraham's bosom: and the rich man also died, and was buried. And in Hades he lifted up his eyes, being in torments, and seeth Abraham afar off, and Lazarus in his bosom. And he cried and said, Father Abraham, have mercy on me, and send Lazarus, that he may dip the tip of his finger in

> water, and cool my tongue; for I am in anguish in this flame.(Luke 16:19-24)

> And when he opened the fourth seal, I heard the voice of the fourth living creature saying, Come. And I saw, and behold, a pale horse: and he that sat upon him, his name was Death; and Hades followed with him. And there was given unto them authority over the fourth part of the earth, to kill with sword, and with famine, and with death, and by the wild beasts of the earth. (Revelation 6:7-8)

> And the sea gave up the dead that were in it; and death and Hades gave up the dead that were in them: and they were judged every man according to their works. And death and Hades were cast into the lake of fire. This is the second death, even the lake of fire. And if any was not found written in the book of life, he was cast into the lake of fire. (Revelation 20:13-15)

There are two places disclosed above that state where a man's spirit can go when his spirit leaves his body. One of them is Paradise, the other is Hades. The Book of Life mentioned above was written before the foundation of the world. John wrote,

> The beast that thou sawest was, and is not; and is about to come up out of the abyss, and to go into perdition. And they that dwell on the earth shall wonder, they whose name hath not been written in the book of life from the foundation of the world, when they behold the beast, how that he was, and is not, and shall come. (Revelation 17:8)

The Book of Life that was written before the foundation of the world is mentioned in the Psalms, and it is that book that contains the names of all the righteous, "Let them be blotted out of the book of life, and not be written with the righteous" (Psalms 69:28).

It is a mystery how a book containing the names of all the saved could have been written before the foundation of the world, but God knows all things and it is He who wrote the book. John wrote,

> But thou hast a few names in Sardis that did not defile their garments: and they shall walk with me in white; for they are worthy. He that overcometh shall thus be arrayed in white garments; and I will in no wise blot his name out of the book of life, and I will confess his name before my Father, and before his angels. (Revelation 3:4-5)

The Book of Life must have had the names of everyone who would ever live written in it if it was written before God created the world. That means a person's name was written in the Book of Life before they were born, but if that person sins then their name would be blotted out of the Book.

Paul knew about the Book of Life and he even knew some of the names that were written in it, he wrote, "I exhort Euodia, and I exhort Syntyche, to be of the same mind in the Lord. Yea, I beseech thee also, true yokefellow, help these women, for they labored with me in the gospel, with Clement also, and the rest of my fellow-workers, whose names are in the book of life" (Philippians 4:2-3).

When a person dies and their name is written in the Book of Life they go to Paradise, the eternal abode of the living. If their name is not written in the Book of Life, then they are in the Book of the Dead, and they enter Hades. John wrote, "And if any was not found written in the book of life, he was cast into the lake of fire" (Revelation 20:15). The Book of the Dead is not mentioned by name in the Bible, but it does exist. John wrote,

> And I saw the dead, the great and the small, standing before the throne; and books were opened: and another book was opened, which is the book of life: and the dead were judged out of the things which were written in the books, according to their works. (Revelation 20:12)

John said that the books were opened, and then another book was opened, and that is at least three books. One of them must have been the Word of God, the Bible, another was the Book of Life, and the third book was the Book of the Dead. The Bible is the Standard that was written by the Lord Himself so men would know how to live and please God, and not sin, and it is that Book that determines a person's judgment. When men live according to that Standard their names are written in the Book of Life. The Book of Life contains the names and the works of all the righteous, the Book of the Dead contains the names and the works of all the lost.

When Jesus died and His spirit went to Hades his Father promised Him that he would not be left there. Luke wrote,

> Being therefore a prophet, and knowing that God had sworn with an oath to him, that of the fruit of his loins he would set one upon his throne; he foreseeing this spake of the resurrection of the Christ, that neither was he left unto Hades, nor did his flesh see corruption. This Jesus did God raise up, whereof we all are witnesses" (Acts 2:30-32).

It is strange to even think that such a powerful force as death and Hades could be abolished. It is even stranger to think that death could be turned into a victory (1 Corinthians 15:54–57). But when Jesus abolished death he abolished the power of death along with it, which is the law and sin (1 Corinthians 15:55–58). By abolishing law, sin, and death, Jesus destroyed the power of the devil. John wrote,

> Every one that doeth sin doeth also lawlessness; and sin is lawlessness. And ye know that he was manifested to take away sins; and in him is no sin. Whosoever abideth in him sinneth not: whosoever sinneth hath not seen him, neither knoweth him. My little children, let no man lead you astray: he that doeth righteousness is righteous, even as he is righteous: he that doeth sin is of the devil; for the devil sinneth from the beginning. To this end was the Son of God manifested, that he might destroy the works of the devil. Whosoever is begotten of God doeth no sin, because his seed abideth in him: and he cannot sin, because he is begotten of God. (1 John 3:4–9)

The reason Christians cannot sin, and they cannot die, is because Jesus has abolished law, sin, and death by his cross and resurrection. Paul wrote, “For sin shall not have dominion over you: for ye are not under law, but under grace” (Romans 6:14). But we know that Christians can sin, and we also know that they can die. However, when a Christian is walking in the light by keeping his faith in Jesus, and always trusting his Father, though he might sin that sin is never charged against him, it is forgiven, and so it is exactly the same as if he had not sinned at all. His sin was immediately forgiven and forgotten (John 1:29). That was all made possible by God’s love and Jesus’ cross. When a believing

Christian sins when he is trying so hard not to, his prayer should be: Father, I thank you for your forgiveness—rather than Father, please forgive me.

We can believe the promises of Jesus and that his promises are faithful and true. We can be assured that when we leave this world we have another world that is much greater and better, and it is forever in the eternal kingdom of God, and it is called heaven. It is there where we shall live in a perfect world forever with the Father, the Son, the Spirit, the angels, and all the brethren who have been saved and have been delivered from death. It has been asked if we shall know each other in the next world, in heaven; shall we know our friends and brothers in the next world, those whom we love and know in this world? It seems clear that we shall most certainly know each other just as we know them now, in this world. Why not? God knows them in both worlds and he calls them by their names. Is it possible in the next world, which is not like this world, that we could have miraculous knowledge and we will not only know those we have had as friends in this physical world, but we will know every living soul who dwells in the spiritual heavenly world? Just something to think about.

The world we live in now has many, many living creatures in it and they have a purpose: they declare the glory of God, and God loves each and every one of them. But they are also for the benefit of men; men love animals and men and animals can form a bond for each other that is as strong as the bond between men. Animals have spirits that keep their bodies alive just as humans do; Solomon said he did not know what happened to those spirits when they left their bodies, but they go somewhere (Ecclesiastes 3:21).

When a person believes in God, in Jesus His Son, and in the Holy Spirit who is our Counselor and Comforter, he can believe that all the promises Jesus made to us are true, and summed up, those promises are perfect eternal life in a perfect world that will never end.

CHAPTER 4

The Price God Paid to Abolish Death an Redeem His Creation—The Three Days of the Cross

THE DAY OF THE cross was the most tragic day, and yet it was the most glorious day in the history of God's creation. It was tragic because an innocent man was crucified for being who he claimed to be, and who He truly was. Jesus was crucified for claiming to be the Son of God. John wrote, "For this cause therefore the Jews sought the more to kill him, because he not only brake the sabbath, but also called God his own Father, making himself equal with God" (John 5:18).

> The Jews therefore came round about him, and said unto him, How long dost thou hold us in suspense? If thou art the Christ, tell us plainly. Jesus answered them, I told you, and ye believe not: the works that I do in my Father's name, these bear witness of me. But ye believe not, because ye are

> not of my sheep. My sheep hear my voice, and I know them, and they follow me: and I give unto them eternal life; and they shall never perish, and no one shall snatch them out of my hand. My Father, who hath given them unto me, is greater than all; and no one is able to snatch them out of the Father's hand. I and the Father are one. The Jews took up stones again to stone him. Jesus answered them, Many good works have I showed you from the Father; for which of those works do ye stone me? The Jews answered him, For a good work we stone thee not, but for blasphemy; and because that thou, being a man, makest thyself God. (John 10:24–33)

Truly Jesus was God, and He was also the Son of God, and He came into the world to tell men about his Father and his Father's love for all men. Jesus said,

> And no one hath ascended into heaven, but he that descended out of heaven, even the Son of man, who is in heaven. And as Moses lifted up the serpent in the wilderness, even so must the Son of man be lifted up; that whosoever believeth may in him have eternal life. For God so loved the world, that he gave his only begotten Son, that whosoever believeth on him should not perish, but have eternal life. For God sent not the Son into the world to judge the world; but that the world should be saved through him. He that believeth on him is not judged: he that believeth not hath been judged already, because he hath not believed on the name of the only begotten Son of God. And this is the judgment, that the light is

> come into the world, and men loved the darkness rather than the light; for their works were evil. For every one that doeth evil hateth the light, and cometh not to the light, lest his works should be reproved. (John 3:13–20)

Jesus came into the world to teach all men that by believing in the Father and His Son they could be forgiven of their sins and enter into eternal life. Jesus said,

> For as the Father raiseth the dead and giveth them life, even so the Son also giveth life to whom he will. For neither doth the Father judge any man, but he hath given all judgment unto the Son; that all may honor the Son, even as they honor the Father. He that honoreth not the Son honoreth not the Father that sent him. Verily, verily, I say unto you, He that heareth my word, and believeth him that sent me, hath eternal life, and cometh not into judgment, but hath passed out of death into life. Verily, verily, I say unto you, The hour cometh, and now is, when the dead shall hear the voice of the Son of God; and they that hear shall live. (John 5:21-25)

For teaching the doctrine that would save men from sin, death, and judgment he was crucified. Jesus said,

> Verily, verily, I say unto you, If a man keep my word, he shall never see death. The Jews said unto him, Now we know that thou hast a demon. Abraham died, and the prophets; and thou sayest, If a man keep my word, he shall never taste of death. Art thou greater than our father Abraham,

> who died? and the prophets died: whom makest thou thyself? Jesus answered, If I glorify myself, my glory is nothing: it is my Father that glorifieth me; of whom ye say, that he is your God; and ye have not known him: but I know him; and if I should say, I know him not, I shall be like unto you, a liar: but I know him, and keep his word. Your father Abraham rejoiced to see my day; and he saw it, and was glad. The Jews therefore said unto him, Thou art not yet fifty years old, and hast thou seen Abraham? Jesus said unto them, Verily, verily, I say unto you, Before Abraham was born, I am. They took up stones therefore to cast at him: but Jesus hid himself, and went out of the temple. (John 8:51–59)

But the day of the cross was also the most glorious of all days, because it was the very special day the Father prepared in his mind before the foundation of the world; it was the day when sin would be punished and abolished and when sinners would be forgiven and set free from law, sin, and death. Sin is never forgiven, it is always punished. It is the sinner who is forgiven. It was the day of the cross that all sins received their just recompense and were punished while the sinners were forgiven and set free (Galatians 5:1). But men receive this wonderful gift only when they believe in Jesus and repent of their past way of living and turn to God and to Jesus' cross for forgiveness.

There have been times when God's wrath was strongly poured out against sin and rebellion, but never had God's wrath been vented against sin in a greater measure than it was on the day of the cross. It was about 1,656 years after God created the world that His wrath against violence and evil was so strongly declared against the world that all mankind perished in a world that was inundated with water, for they had become very wicked indeed. Moses wrote,

> And Jehovah saw that the wickedness of man was great in the earth, and that every imagination of the thoughts of his heart was only evil continually. And it repented Jehovah that he had made man on the earth, and it grieved him at his heart. And Jehovah said, I will destroy man whom I have created from the face of the ground; both man, and beast, and creeping things, and birds of the heavens; for it repenteth me that I have made them. (Genesis 6:5–7)

It is sad the entire creation and all living creatures in it had to suffer and die for the sins of men, but that happened because of the infinite hatred God has for sin. Peter wrote,

> For if God spared not angels when they sinned, but cast them down to hell, and committed them to pits of darkness, to be reserved unto judgment; and spared not the ancient world, but preserved Noah with seven others, a preacher of and turning the cities of Sodom and Gomorrah into ashes condemned them with an overthrow, and delivered righteous Lot, sore distressed by the lascivious life of the wicked (for that righteous man dwelling among them, in seeing and hearing, vexed his righteous soul from day to day with their lawless deeds): the Lord knoweth how to deliver the godly out of temptation, and to keep the unrighteous under punishment unto the day of judgment. (2 Peter 2:4-9)

Only Noah was found righteous and he and his family were spared from the great flood that covered the earth and destroyed all living creatures. Moses wrote,

> Fifteen cubits upward did the waters prevail; and the mountains were covered. And all flesh died that moved upon the earth, both birds, and cattle, and beasts, and every creeping thing that creepeth upon the earth, and every man: all in hose nostrils was the breath of the spirit of life, of all that was on the dry land, died. And every living thing was destroyed that was upon the face of the ground, both man, and cattle, and creeping things, and birds of the heavens; and they were destroyed from the earth: and Noah only was left, and they that were with him in the ark. And the waters prevailed upon the earth a hundred and fifty days. (Genesis 7:20-24)

There was another occasion when God's wrath fell so very heavily on sinful men that it completely destroyed their cities. That was the day God destroyed Sodom and Gomorrah, the five cities of the plains (Genesis 18:20; 19:23–25). Peter said God's anger was so great against those cities that he turned them to ashes. Peter wrote, "and turning the cities of Sodom and Gomorrah into ashes condemned them with an overthrow, having made them an example unto those that should live ungodly" (2Peter 2:6). Crystalized gold has been found in the ruins of those cities, and it takes 6,000 degrees temperature to cause that, and that is hotter than the surface of the sun.

But never has God's wrath been poured out in any stronger measure against sin than it was poured out on the day Jesus died on the cross. It was that day God punished sin once for all. It was the day that God dealt with all the problems and devastation that sin had caused. It was Jesus who took God's wrath upon himself and paid the price God demanded so all sinners could be forgiven. Matthew and Luke described the day Jesus died on the cross vividly.

> Now from the sixth hour there was darkness over all the land until the ninth hour. And about the ninth hour Jesus cried with a loud voice, saying, Eli, Eli, lama sabachthani? that is, My God, my God, why hast thou forsaken me? And some of them stood there, when they heard it, said, This man calleth Elijah. And straightway one of them ran, and took a sponge, and filled it with vinegar, and put it on a reed, and gave him to drink. And the rest said, Let be; let us see whether Elijah cometh to save him. And Jesus cried again with a loud voice, and yielded up his spirit. And behold, the veil of the temple was rent in two from the top to the bottom; and the earth did quake; and the rocks were rent; and the tombs were opened; and many bodies of the saints that had fallen asleep were raised. (Matthew 27:45–52)

> And it was now about the sixth hour, and a darkness came over the whole land until the ninth hour, the sun's light failing: and the veil of the temple was rent in the midst. And Jesus, crying with a loud voice, said, Father, into thy hands I commend my spirit: and having said this, he gave up the ghost. And when the centurion saw what was done, he glorified God, saying, Certainly this was a righteous man. And all the multitudes that came together to this sight, when they beheld

> the things that were done, returned smiting their breasts. (Luke 23:44–48)

It was not those who were crucifying Jesus who were the object of God's wrath because they were crucifying his Son. It was the one who was being crucified who was suffering the agony of God's wrath. God was punishing sin, and it was Jesus who was taking that punishment upon himself, because for him to save the world from sin and death that was the price he must pay—the punishment that should have fallen upon the people who had committed the terrible acts of aggression against his Father all fell upon the Son, and he was paying the price necessary to take them all away.

Paul wrote that Jesus was willing to be made sin for us so we could be saved. He wrote, "Him who knew no sin he made to be sin on our behalf; that we might become the righteousness of God in him" (2 Corinthians 5:21). There are some who find it impossible to believe that the Almighty who left his throne of glory and became the Son of man could actually have been made to be sin by God himself, and so they change it to *sin-offering*. There are some who feel that it would not be possible for God to actually forsake his own Son, or for Jesus to have to go into Hades and be cut off from God and the land of the living to pay for our sins. The only reason for that kind of thinking is because it just expects just a little too much for the Son of God to have to suffer, especially at the hands of his Father. But since that is what the scriptures say, that is what must have happened. All of this just describes how greatly Jesus was willing to suffer and the tremendous price He was willing to pay to become our Savior. It is best not to go by our feelings and emotions and change the scriptures to suit them. It is best to accept what the scriptures say word for word, and then change our feelings and emotions to accept exactly what the Bible teaches, just as it was written.

The punishment Jesus was willing to suffer for us, and the chastisement he was willing to take upon himself for our sins, is beyond our greatest imagination. What God hated most, sin, he actually and personally became for us in his Son so that we might be saved, and that we might be delivered from the wrath of God, which is death. Such love is so great it is far beyond human comprehension.

Once we were delivered from sin and its power Jesus made us as righteous as God himself is righteous. All of that was actually accomplished by the way of the cross. That is how much love God has for us. Paul wrote,

> For while we were yet weak, in due season Christ died for the ungodly. For scarcely for a righteous man will one die: for peradventure for the good man some one would even dare to die. But God commendeth his own love toward us, in that, while we were yet sinners, Christ died for us. Much more then, being now justified by his blood, shall we be saved from the wrath of God through him. For if, while we were enemies, we were reconciled to God through the death of his Son, much more, being reconciled, shall we be saved by his life; and not only so, but we also rejoice in God through our Lord Jesus Christ, through whom we have now received the reconciliation. (Romans 5:6–11)

Jesus' body was taken down from the cross and buried in a new tomb where no man had ever been laid. Isaiah wrote, "And they made his grave with the wicked, and with a rich man in his death; although he had done no violence, neither was any deceit in his mouth" (Isaiah 53:9). It is interesting how accurately

Isaiah predicted in such detail what would happen at the cross several hundred years before it occurred. John wrote,

> And there came also Nicodemus, he who at the first came to him by night, bringing a mixture of myrrh and aloes, about a hundred pounds. So they took the body of Jesus, and bound it in linen cloths with the spices, as the custom of the Jews is to bury. Now in the place where he was crucified there was a garden; and in the garden a new tomb wherein was never man yet laid. There then because of the Jews' Preparation (for the tomb was nigh at hand) they laid Jesus. (John 19:39–42)

There was a reason for Jesus being buried in a new tomb. When the disciples went to the tomb to anoint Jesus' body, and there was none, they did not have to count bodies to see if it was Jesus' body that was missing. Also, when the women arrived at the tomb, the first thing they saw was that the stone had been rolled away from the entrance to the tomb. They entered the tomb, and Jesus was not there. The stone was not rolled away so Jesus could escape; it was rolled away so the women could enter the tomb and see that Jesus was not there. (Luke 24:1–3). Jesus' body was in the tomb three days. But where were his soul and his spirit while his body was in the tomb?

When Jesus died on the cross he took the full punishment for all sin upon himself, both physically and spiritually. Jesus died the same death that a sinner dies if that sinner dies in his sins, and without his sins being forgiven.

It was Adam who brought sin and death into the world, and men die physically because of Adam's sin. Little babies die, but they have never sinned. Little babies suffer death as a consequence of Adam's transgression, just as all living things suffer death because of Adam's sin. But men die spiritually for their own sins. Romans 6:23 says, "For the wages of sin is death; but the free gift of God is eternal life in Christ Jesus our Lord." Ezekiel 18:20 says, "The soul that sinneth, it shall die: the son shall not bear the iniquity of the father, neither shall the father bear the iniquity of the son; the righteousness of the righteous shall be upon him, and the wickedness of the wicked shall be upon him."

Physical death is the separation of the spirit and the soul from the body. That occurs the moment the spirit leaves the body (James 2:26). Spiritual death, when the soul dies, is when it is separated from God because of sin, and it is cut off out of the land of the living. For Jesus to pay fully for our sins he had to experience the death of a sinner; He must die both physically and spiritually though he had no sin. Therefore, Jesus cry from the cross when he was dying, "My God, My God, why have you forsaken me?" had a true and real meaning, for God had forsaken him because he had been made to be sin so we could be made righteous (2 Corinthians 5:21). That is when God saw the agony of His soul, and was satisfied (Isaiah 53:11), and when He poured out his soul unto death (Isaiah 53:12).

When Jesus was made to be sin it was sin that was nailed to the cross, and when he died it was sin that died. When Jesus was forsaken of God it was sin that was forsaken of God and punished. Jesus was willing to bear all the grief and pain that sin had caused and take that burden upon himself so we could be saved. That is how much God loves us. But where did Jesus' spirit go when he was forsaken of God?

It is a shame there are people who have been raised in a religious environment in which they are taught, "This is the way it is, this is the way it has always been, and this is the way it will always be—don't question it." That philosophy leaves little room for a person to grow up and study the Bible on their own initiative and think for themselves, and arrive at their own conclusion as to what the scriptures actually teach. A person who has been raised under the above way of thinking will study the Bible to prove what they already believe rather than with the purpose of studying it to discover what it actually teaches.

There are times when a person comes to a scripture that is very difficult to understand, like Romans chapter 5, and even the apostle Peter realized that. He said,

> Wherefore, beloved, seeing that ye look for these things, give diligence that ye may be found in peace, without spot and blameless in his sight. And account that the longsuffering of our Lord is salvation; even as our beloved brother Paul also, according to the wisdom given to him, wrote unto you; as also in all his epistles, speaking in them of these things; wherein are some things hard to be understood, which the ignorant and unstedfast wrest, as they do also the other scriptures, unto their own destruction. (2 Peter 3:14–16).

Maybe the real meaning that a scripture plainly teaches is something a person does not want to believe because it just does not seem possible or reasonable. It might be because it is against what they have been taught. But when it is evident that a scripture means just exactly what It says, and says exactly what it means, then that is the way it should be accepted.

It is reasonable that we should study the Bible and come to our own conclusions as to what it means. But we should be ready and willing to change our way of thinking about how we interpret the Bible when we see there is the possibility we might be wrong in our way of thinking. It is very good to study the Bible with other people, and especially when we are viewing a very difficult part of the Bible that is difficult to understand, and then compare notes. But we should be leery of anyone we study the

Bible with when they tell us, "*I know that is what it seems to say, but let me tell you what it really means*."

We should stand fast on what we believe to be the truth and not change our way of thinking at all unless we see a very good reason to do so. Jesus is Lord, and he died on the cross to save us from law, sin, and death, and that point is not debatable; but there are other facts in the Bible that are not so firm. To be able to study the Bible using the above approach requires wisdom, maturity, patience, and understanding.

When the Bible was translated into English the words the translators used to compose our English Bible (and there were many translators, something like fifty-seven, all experts in their field) were chosen very carefully. If after a scriptures had been translated and accepted, and by chance one of the words just did not seem to be the exact word that should have been used, it took two-thirds of the translating committee to make the change. When I am in a Bible class, and a person makes the comment that a word they don't like is a *bad translation*, I just cringe. Do they actually know more about how the Bible should have been translated than the translators who translated it, and they knew all the languages used in the translation equally well? This does not apply to transliterations, or to paraphrasing the Bible. I also feel uncomfortable when I read the Bible in class, and it has a perfectly clear and obvious meaning, but because of personal reasons and preferences a person changes the meaning to make it fit what they already believe, or what they want to believe. What follows is the reason I have made the above observation.

I love to study the Bible with people who do not see the Bible the way I see it, especially when it is a passage of scripture that is very difficult to understand. I feel there is always the possibility that I might be in the wrong, and that I might learn something from someone else's viewpoint. Giving thanks to God I have had that experience many times. Maybe we all need to have the attitude Paul said the church in Beroea had. Luke wrote,

> And the brethren immediately sent away Paul and Silas by night unto Beroea: who when they were come thither went into the synagogue of the Jews. Now these were more noble than those in Thessalonica, in that they received the word with all readiness of the mind, examining the Scriptures daily, whether these things were so. (Acts 17:10–11)

One of the areas in the Bible where there are different points of view is where Jesus was and what he did the three days his body was in the tomb. There are some who are terribly offended at even the suggestion that when Jesus' Spirit left his body he actually, of his own volition, went into Hades, the realm of the dead. However, the Bible is very plain but very brief about what happened those three days. Jesus said himself that he must spend three days and three nights in the heart of the earth. Jesus said,

> But he answered and said unto them, An evil and adulterous generation seeketh after a sign; and there shall no sign be given it but the sign of Jonah the prophet: for as Jonah was three days and three nights in the belly of the whale; so shall the Son of man be three days and three nights in the heart of the earth. (Matthew 12:39–40)

What Jesus said means much more than just his body being in the tomb three days and three nights. It was not just Jonah's body that was in the belly of a whale, it was all of Jonah. Paul also spoke of this,

> But unto each one of us was the grace given according to the measure of the gift of Christ. Wherefore he saith, When he ascended on high,

> he led captivity captive, and gave gifts unto men. (Now this, He ascended, what is it but that he also descended into the lower parts of the earth? He that descended is the same also that ascended far above all the heavens, that he might fill all things). (Ephesians 4:7–10)

The same Jesus that ascended into heaven is the same Jesus that descended into the lower parts of the earth. That is the place where rebellious angels were sent to be punished for their disobedience against God. Peter wrote, "For if God spared not angels when they sinned, but cast them down to hell, and committed them to pits of darkness, to be reserved unto judgment..." (2 Peter 2:4). Jude wrote, "And angels that kept not their own principality, but left their proper habitation, he hath kept in everlasting bonds under darkness unto the judgment of the great day" (Jude 1:6). Psalms 63:8–10 says, "My soul followeth hard after thee: Thy right hand upholdeth me. But those that seek my soul, to destroy it, Shall go into the lower parts of the earth. They shall be given over to the power of the sword: They shall be a portion for foxes."

Isaiah chapter 53 is a chapter in the Bible that describes the sacrifice of Jesus and the day of the cross very clearly. Isaiah said that Jesus took all of the grief, all the guilt, and all the punishment that was going to fall upon sinners—upon himself—and he was smitten for the transgressions that others had committed. That chapter describes the spiritual punishment Jesus suffered for sin which was the pouring out His soul unto death, and being cut off out of the land of the living. Isaiah wrote,

> Surely he hath borne our griefs, and carried our sorrows; yet we did esteem him stricken, smitten of God, and afflicted. But he was wounded for our transgressions, he was bruised for our iniquities;

> the chastisement of our peace was upon him; and with his stripes we are healed. All we like sheep have gone astray; we have turned every one to his own way; and Jehovah hath laid on him the iniquity of us all. He was oppressed, yet when he was afflicted he opened not his mouth; as a lamb that is led to the slaughter, and as a sheep that before its shearers is dumb, so he opened not his mouth. By oppression and judgment he was taken away; and as for his generation, who among them considered that he was cut off out of the land of the living for the transgression of my people to whom the stroke was due? Therefore will I divide him a portion with the great, and he shall divide the spoil with the strong; because he poured out his soul unto death, and was numbered with the transgressors: yet he bare the sin of many, and made intercession for the transgressors. (53:4–12)

Where did Jesus go when he was cut off out of the land of the living? Where was he when he had been numbered with the transgressors who had committed the acts of rebellion against his God for which he was suffering? What happened to Jesus when he poured out his soul unto death; when his soul died? They were the ones upon whom the stroke of death should have fallen, but instead that stroke fell upon Jesus. When Jesus died and his body was placed in the tomb that was not Jesus being cut off out of the land of the living. This world is not the land of the living (Galatians 1:4). Jesus was cut off out of the land of the living when he poured out his soul unto death. Isaiah wrote,

> Yet it pleased Jehovah to bruise him; he hath put him to grief: when thou shalt make his soul an

> offering for sin, he shall see his seed, he shall prolong his days, and the pleasure of Jehovah shall prosper in his hand. He shall see of the travail of his soul, and shall be satisfied: by the knowledge of himself shall my righteous servant justify many; and he shall bear their iniquities. Therefore will I divide him a portion with the great, and he shall divide the spoil with the strong; because he poured out his soul unto death, and was numbered with the transgressors: yet he bare the sin of many, and made intercession for the transgressors. (Isaiah 53:10–12)

The land of the living is where God lives. Psalms 27:13 says, "I had fainted, unless I had believed to see the goodness of Jehovah In the land of the living." Psalms 116:9 says, "I will walk before Jehovah In the land of the living." Psalms 142:5 says, "I cried unto thee, O Jehovah; I said, Thou art my refuge, my portion in the land of the living."

Maybe anyone who feels that it is asking just a little too much to believe Jesus actually went into Hades to spiritually pay for our sins should also consider that it might be asking a little too much of the Almighty Jehovah God himself to leave his throne of glory and his inapproachable light, to give up his equality with God, and come into this world to be spit on, beaten, blasphemed, mocked, crowned with thorns, and nailed to a cross to be left to die (Matthew 27:26–31)—but most all Christians accept that, because that is exactly what he did.

In Acts chapter 2, Jesus was promised by his Father that his body would not be left in the grave long enough to see corruption, nor would his soul be left in Hades. Therefore, his body had to be in the grave, and his soul had to be in Hades for those promises to mean anything to Him. Luke wrote,

Ye men of Israel, hear these words: Jesus of Nazareth, a man approved of God unto you by mighty works and wonders and signs which God did by him in the midst of you, even as ye yourselves know; him, being delivered up by the determinate counsel and foreknowledge of God, ye by the hand of lawless men did crucify and slay: whom God raised up, having loosed the pangs of death: because it was not possible that he should be holden of it. For David saith concerning him, I beheld the Lord always before my face; For he is on my right hand, that I should not be moved: Therefore my heart was glad, and my tongue rejoiced; Moreover my flesh also shall dwell in hope: Because thou wilt not leave my soul unto Hades, Neither wilt thou give thy Holy One to see corruption. Thou madest known unto me the ways of life; Thou shalt make me full of gladness with thy countenance. Brethren, I may say unto you freely of the patriarch David, that he both died and was buried, and his tomb is with us unto this day. Being therefore a prophet, and knowing that God had sworn with an oath to him, that of the fruit of his loins he would set one upon his throne; he foreseeing this spake of the resurrection of the Christ, that neither was he left unto Hades, nor did his flesh see corruption. This Jesus did God raise up, whereof we all are witnesses. Being therefore by the right hand of God exalted, and having received of the Father the promise of the Holy Spirit, he hath poured forth this, which ye see and hear. (Acts 2:22–33 says)

Those promises were precious to Jesus because he had given up his equality with God when he became the Son of man (Philippians 2:5–8), and therefore Jesus had no more power over death or Hades than any other man had. When Jesus went into the grave, and his human Spirit went into Hades, his only hope of escaping those dreadful places was by trusting in the faithfulness of his Father, and his Father's promises. What makes this so very precious to us is—we rely on those same promises! Our resurrection from the grave depends on the same promise that Jesus' Father made to him, to raise him from the tomb. Therefore our resurrection is just as certain for us as Jesus' resurrection was for him; except we shall never have to enter Hades because Jesus went there for us.

There is a scripture in Matthew that affirms how strongly Jesus believed in his Father's promises. Matthew 16:13–19 says,

> Now when Jesus came into the parts of Caesarea Philippi, he asked his disciples, saying, Who do men say that the Son of man is? And they said, Some say John the Baptist; some, Elijah; and others, Jeremiah, or one of the prophets. He saith unto them, But who say ye that I am? And Simon Peter answered and said, Thou art the Christ, the Son of the living God. And Jesus answered and said unto him, Blessed art thou, Simon Bar-Jonah: for flesh and blood hath not revealed it unto thee, but my Father who is in heaven. And I also say unto thee, that thou art Peter, and upon this rock I will build my church; and the gates of Hades shall not prevail against it. I will give unto thee the keys of the kingdom of heaven: and whatsoever thou shalt bind on earth shall be bound in heaven; and whatsoever thou shalt loose on earth shall be loosed in heaven.

Jesus said the gates of Hades shall not stop him from building his church. He did not say some terrible and powerful evil force would stop him, but only some gates. What is the function of a gate? How could a gate, any gate, prevail against Jesus building his church? A gate has only one function, and that function is control. A gate controls entrance or exit to some regulated place. The gates of Hades only open one way, and that way is to allow entrance. Since it is the gates to Hades that Jesus said could not prevent him from building his church it must mean that those gates could never hold him to and prevent his escape to keep him from building his church. At the appointed time of his Father Jesus would exit Hades and his Spirit and Soul would return to his body. That would cause his resurrection and his body would come out of the grave and live again. It was in the same body that was crucified in which Jesus would return to his disciples and live with them for forty days. It was the same body in which he would build his church and then in which he would ascend into heaven. Luke wrote in his gospel,

> And he said unto them, Why are ye troubled? and wherefore do questionings arise in your heart? See my hands and my feet, that it is I myself: handle me, and see; for a spirit hath not flesh and bones, as ye behold me having. And when he had said this, he showed them his hands and his feet. And while they still disbelieved for joy, and wondered, he said unto them, Have ye here anything to eat? And they gave him a piece of a broiled fish. (Luke 24:38–42)

There was another apostle, Thomas, who refused to believe Jesus had actually been raised from the tomb, and he said he would not believe until he saw and touched the risen Lord. John wrote,

> But Thomas, one of the twelve, called Didymus, was not with them when Jesus came. The other disciples therefore said unto him, We have seen the Lord. But he said unto them, Except I shall see in his hands the print of the nails, and put my hand into his side, I will not believe. And after eight days again his disciples were within, and Thomas with them. Jesus cometh, the doors being shut, and stood in the midst, and said, Peace be unto you. Then saith he to Thomas, Reach hither thy finger, and see my hands; and reach hither thy hand, and put it into my side: and be not faithless, but believing. Thomas answered and said unto him, My Lord and my God. Jesus saith unto him, Because thou hast seen me, thou hast believed: blessed are they that have not seen, and yet have believed. (John 20:24-29)

There is an interesting scripture in First Peter that explains what Jesus did while he was in Hades. Peter wrote,

> For it is better, if the will of God should so will, that ye suffer for well-doing than for evil-doing. Because Christ also suffered for sins once, the righteous for the unrighteous, that he might bring us to God; being put to death in the flesh, but made alive in the spirit; in which also he went and preached unto the spirits in prison, that aforetime were disobedient, when the longsuffering of God waited in the days of Noah, while the ark was a preparing, wherein few, that is, eight souls, were saved through water: which also after a true likeness doth now save you, even baptism, not the putting away of the filth of the flesh, but the

> interrogation of a good conscience toward God, through the resurrection of Jesus Christ; who is on the right hand of God, having gone into heaven; angels and authorities and powers being made subject unto him. (1 Peter 3:17-22)

This is a strange and difficult of scripture. All we can know about it is what is written here, and also what Peter wrote in 1 Peter 4:5–6, just a few verses ahead; therefore these difficult scriptures are speaking of the same event. Peter wrote,

> For the time past may suffice to have wrought the desire of the Gentiles, and to have walked in lasciviousness, lusts, winebibbings, revellings, carousings, and abominable idolatries: wherein they think strange that ye run not with them into the same excess of riot, speaking evil of you: who shall give account to him that is ready to judge the living and the dead. For unto this end was the gospel preached even to the dead, that they might be judged indeed according to men in the flesh, but live according to God in the spirit. (1 Peter 3:3-6)

First, Peter said that it was the Spirit of Jesus who preached to the spirits in prison (1 Peter 3:19). Then Peter said it was the gospel that was preached even to the dead (1 Peter 4:6). The spirits in prison, and the dead spirits to whom the gospel was preached, were all the same spirits, they were dead spirits in prison that had died in the flood. It was the gospel that was preached to the dead and therefore it was the gospel that was preached to the spirits in prison, and it was Jesus who was the preacher, and He is the only one who could have done that.

Jesus was not forced into Hades; He was not carried off by the angles and cast into that dreadful place. He went there himself, of his own volition, just as he delivered himself up to be crucified of his own volition. Jesus entered that dreadful place knowing that it was by the promise of his Father he would not be left there. It is astonishing that Jesus could leave the cross in his Spirit and enter that horrible place of death and suffering. It is also amazing that when the promise of his father was fulfilled the gates of Hades could not hold him in. Jesus went into Hades to pay for our sins. When he left Hades he left our sins in that appalling place, a place that is as far away from us as east is from west. Psalms103:12 says, "As far as the east is from the west, So far hath he removed our transgressions from us." It might be possible to measure the distance from north to south, the poles, but not from east to west, for that measurement is not imaginable.

But there are questions: Why would Jesus preach to dead spirits in prison, or Hades, when there was no hope of escape from that horrible place? Why did he preach only to those who had died in the 120 year period of the flood while Noah was building the ark? How could the Spirit of Jesus be made alive? It was Jesus' human Spirit that died when he was forsaken by God, and it was made alive when he left the cross, because a living spirit cannot be made alive, it is alive. Only a dead spirit can be made alive. Therefore it was not the Holy Spirit but the human spirit of Jesus that was made alive.

There are no answers to those questions anywhere in the Bible, except in Isaiah, chapter 53. IIowever, according to what is written in the book: The Genesis Flood, by John C. Whitcomb and Henry Morris, the very most conservative estimate for the population of the world in the year 1656 after the creation (about 2,400 years B.C.—the year of the flood), was one 1,030,000,000 people. That is about what the population of the earth was in the year 1,800. The population of the world when God destroyed it with the flood could have been as great as it is today. The reason for that is because, before the flood, people lived for some nine-hundred years, and longer. Maybe when God saw so many perish in such a violent manner that he had a plan to offer them mercy and another chance—a chance to leave that dreadful place called Hades if they would only listen to his Son who was right there with them, and teaching them. If only they would believe the message that Jesus preached to them they could be forgiven, and they could leave that place with Jesus when he left it. The reason the gospel was preached to the dead was so they could hear it and be judged as if they were still alive and living in their flesh and blood bodies. Then, if they believed what they heard they could be made alive and live according to God in the Spirit.

The question is: Does the cross have the power of God that is so mighty that it could have actually extended into Hades at the time when Jesus went there, and could it have offered God's grace, mercy, and forgiveness to those who had perished in the flood? Could it have been possible that if they would just believe what Jesus taught them, the gospel, that He truly was the Son of God, and that He had died on the cross for their sins, and for all sinners, then they could actually escape that dreadful place called Hades and leave it with Jesus when he left? If this did actually happen it would happen only once, because Jesus was crucified only once, and he went to preach to the spirits in prison only once. But he certainly did do it once, the Bible says so. It happened because of the infinite love that God has for his children, whether they were alive and well, or even those who had perished and were among the abode of the dead. It is sad that we don't know if anyone responded to Jesus' preaching, or what resulted from his preaching the gospel to people in prison. Did anyone believe him and leave with him? We just don't know.

Jesus' body died on the cross and was buried. His human Spirit also died when Jesus was forsaken by God (Isaiah 53:11–12; Matthew 27:46) and his spirit was cut off out of the land of the living (Isaiah 53:8, 12). (That is the cup Jesus prayed to God he would not have to drink, and all of this is something that is so infinitely deep and so far past human comprehension that it can never be fully understood, but it can be accepted by faith).

What we are looking at is what it cost God to forgive us of our sins and abolish death, and what Jesus was willing to do to correct all the problems sin had instigated, and pay for the damage sin had caused; and then redeem and restore the creation back to God. Jesus never sinned, and so the death he suffered, physically and spiritually, was for Adam's sin, and for all sin. For us to be perfectly set free from sin and death full payment had to be made to satisfy both deaths, both spiritual death and physical death (Romans 3:23–26). Jesus paid that price in full when he took the punishment that was due to fall upon sinners upon himself. We truly have been set free from sin, death, and law, by Jesus and his cross.

It is difficult to understand when Jesus' Spirit was made alive. Was it before he went into Hades, or when he left Hades? If his Spirit was made alive before he went into Hades, he would be the only living spirit in the realm of the dead. That would have made a tremendous impression upon those in Hades to whom Jesus preached the gospel. That must mean that when Jesus died on the cross, and in his spirit he went to preach to the spirits in prison, not only was God's mercy and grace being offered to all who lived over the entire face of the earth, offering the forgiveness of sin and eternal life to all men; but God's mercy and grace also went with Jesus into Hades to offer pardon to those who had perished in the flood. It was when Jesus was in Hades that God's grace was extended into the realm of the dead (1 Peter 4:5–6). Why it extended only to those of a 120 year period, or to the time of the flood while Noah was building the ark, is a question only God can answer.

It was the Spirit of God's Son, and not Noah, who preached the gospel to those who were in prison. Noah was a preacher of righteousness (2 Peter 2:5), but here it says it was the Spirit of Christ who was made alive that went and preached to the spirits who were in prison because they had been disobedient in the days of Noah.

The point Peter made is that all men shall stand before God to be judged. Paul wrote, "For we must all be made manifest before the judgment-seat of Christ; that each one may receive the things done in the body, according to what he hath done, whether it be good or bad" (2 Corinthians 5:10). If a person is alive when Jesus comes to judge the world, he shall be judged in his flesh—but if a person had died before Jesus comes, he shall still be judged, for dying does not allow a person to escape the judgment of God (Hebrews 9:27). The message of Peter is that since God is going to judge the living and the dead, the gospel was preached even to the dead, so that those who heard it could escape the punishment they deserved for all of their sins, which is death—a death they had already died. But through the preaching of Jesus and his gospel they could live again, and have eternal life. For some reason God saw fit to allow the gospel to be preached even to the dead—*even* meaning that this was a rare and exceptional case. Paul, and the other apostles had preached the gospel to the whole world of the living in some thirty or forty years after Jesus had died (Colossians 1:3–6). But someone else preached the gospel even to the dead.

CHAPTER 5

What Must One Do to Escape Death and Enter the Eternal Kingdom of Heaven?

IT HAS BEEN SAID that heaven is a prepared place for prepared people, and such is true. It was Jesus who came to prepare a place for God's children because they are His brethren. Jesus said, "In my Father's house are many mansions; if it were not so, I would have told you; for I go to prepare a place for you. And if I go and prepare a place for you, I come again, and will receive you unto myself; that where I am, there ye may be also" (John 14:2-3). When Jesus cleansed God's children from sin by purifying them with his blood he called them his brethren. In Hebrews it is written, "For both he that sanctifieth and they that are sanctified are all of one: for which cause he is not ashamed to call them brethren, saying, I will declare thy name unto my brethren, In the midst of the congregation will I sing thy praise" (Hebrews 2:11-12). Because God's children are the brothers of Christ they shall all be given an equal inheritance with Him. Paul wrote,

> For as many as are led by the Spirit of God, these are sons of God. For ye received not the spirit of bondage again unto fear; but ye received the spirit of adoption, whereby we cry, Abba, Father. The Spirit himself beareth witness with our spirit, that we are children of God: and if children, then heirs; heirs of God, and joint-heirs with Christ; if so be that we suffer with him, that we may be also glorified with him" (Romans 8:14-17).

Jesus is the Heir of all things and therefore so also are his children. It is written in Hebrews, "God, having of old time spoken unto the fathers in the prophets by divers portions and in divers manners, hath at the end of these days spoken unto us in his Son, whom he appointed heir of all things, through whom also he made the worlds" (Hebrews 1:1-2). What a wonderful world the children of God have; they are sons of the almighty God, brothers of their Savior the Lord Jesus Christ, and they are equal heirs of the One who shall inherit everything that belongs to God. God's children shall inherit the kingdom of heaven and it shall be their abode forever, and their place in the world to come has already been prepared for them. It was prepared by the life of their Savior, by his teachings and his example, and by his death on the cross that was the sacrifice that took away the sins of the world and purchased the kingdom of God.

Therefore, it is necessary that the children of God prepare themselves for the place that God has prepared for them, and that way is by obedience to Jesus. John wrote, "Jesus saith unto him, I am the way, and the truth, and the life: no one cometh unto the Father, but by me" (John 14:6). The way to God and entrance into his kingdom is so simple that it cannot be misunderstood. God made it simple so even the simple could understand it and be saved. Mark wrote, "And he said unto them, Go ye into all the world, and preach the gospel to the whole creation. He that believeth and is baptized shall be saved; but he that disbelieveth shall be condemned" (Mark 16:15-16). It does not take a brilliant mind to understand the Word of God and be saved, it takes an understanding heart that is willing to accept the truth that Jesus died on a cross to save the world from sin and death, and when one believes that and they are baptized they shall be saved. Mark wrote, "And he said unto them, Go ye into all the world, and preach the gospel to the whole creation. He that believeth and is baptized shall be saved; but he that disbelieveth shall be condemned" (Mark 16:15-16).

The way to God is so easy to understand that some have difficulty comprehending how such a simple way could be such a marvelous way to such a wonderful blessing as eternal life in a perfect kingdom. All one must do to see such is true is to read about how men were converted and saved as it is written in the Bible. When Paul and Silas were on one of their missionary journeys they entered a town called Philippi. They understood that there was a place by a river there where women gathered together on the Sabbath day to pray and worship God, but they only knew of Moses and the law. Paul went there to teach them about Jesus and his grace. Luke wrote,

> And on the sabbath day we went forth without the gate by a river side, where we supposed there was a place of prayer; and we sat down, and spake unto the women that were come together. And a certain woman named Lydia, a seller of purple of the city of Thyatira, one that worshipped God, heard us: whose heart the Lord opened to give heed unto the things which were spoken by Paul. And when she was baptized, and her household, she besought us, saying, If ye have judged me to be faithful to the Lord, come into my house,

> and abide there. And she constrained us. (Acts 16:13-16)

In just one day, in a matter of hours, and no seminaries or Bible classes involved, Paul taught several ladies about Christ and his kingdom; they believed Paul, they were baptized, and they entered the kingdom God and were saved. Someday maybe we can meet with those ladies just as Paul did.

A little later in the same city Paul preached the gospel to many others. His message was so powerful that he and Silas were beaten, arrested, and taken to prison. The jailer was charged to guard them carefully, for he was told they were very dangerous men. That meant if they escaped the jailer would be beheaded. After they were arrested Luke wrote about what happened to them.

> Setting sail therefore from Troas, we made a straight course to Samothrace, and the day following to Neapolis; And the multitude rose up together against them: and the magistrates rent their garments off them, and commanded to beat them with rods. And when they had laid many stripes upon them, they cast them into prison, charging the jailor to keep them safely: who, having received such a charge, cast them into the inner prison, and made their feet fast in the stocks. But about midnight Paul and Silas were praying and singing hymns unto God, and the prisoners were listening to them; and suddenly there was a great earthquake, so that the foundations of the prison-house were shaken: and immediately all the doors were opened, and every one's bands were loosed. And the jailor, being roused out of sleep and seeing the prison doors open, drew his sword and was about to kill himself, supposing

that the prisoners had escaped. But Paul cried with a loud voice, saying, Do thyself no harm: for we are all here. And he called for lights and sprang in, and, trembling for fear, fell down before Paul and Silas, and brought them out and said, Sirs, what must I do to be saved? And they said, Believe on the Lord Jesus, and thou shalt be saved, thou and thy house. And they spake the word of the Lord unto him, with all that were in his house. And he took them the same hour of the night, and washed their stripes; and was baptized, he and all his, immediately. And he brought them up into his house, and set food before them, and rejoiced greatly, with all his house, having believed in God. But when it was day, the magistrates sent the serjeants, saying, Let those men go. And the jailor reported the words to Paul, saying, The magistrates have sent to let you go: now therefore come forth, and go in peace. But Paul said unto them, They have beaten us publicly, uncondemned, men that are Romans, and have cast us into prison; and do they now cast us out privily? Nay verily; but let them come themselves and bring us out. And the serjeants reported these words unto the magistrates: and they feared when they heard that they were Romans; and they came and besought them; and when they had brought them out, they asked them to go away from the city. And they went out of the prison, and entered into the house of Lydia: and when they had seen the brethren, they comforted them, and departed. (Acts 16:11-40)

Paul was a hard core determined minister and a preacher of the Word, and when he spoke the words of the gospel he was determined that men would listen, and they did; and when he and Silas had been so unjustly arrested and put it prison for preaching the Word he demanded an apology. When Paul and Silas were in the prison singing songs of praise to God, and when God helped them out by creating an earthquake that shook the doors off of the prison, it caused the prison guard to experience such great fear the he fell before the feet of his prisoners and cried out, "sirs, what must I do to be saved?" It was so shocking that even the prisoners staid in the prison rather than quickly running to be free.

The prison guard and his family were baptized and they were saved. There are other accounts in the Bible that illustrate how quickly and how simple it is for one to hear the Word of God and obey it, such as the case of Phillip and the Ethiopian eunuch. God wants his people to hear his word and be saved; he does not one soul to be lost. Paul wrote,

> I exhort therefore, first of all, that supplications, prayers, intercessions, thanksgivings, be made for all men; for kings and all that are in high place; that we may lead a tranquil and quiet life in all godliness and gravity. This is good and acceptable in the sight of God our Saviour; who would have all men to be saved, and come to the knowledge of the truth. (1 Timothy 2:1-4)

Peter wrote, "The Lord is not slack concerning his promise, as some count slackness; but is longsuffering to you-ward, not wishing that any should perish, but that all should come to repentance" (2 Peter 3:9). To illustrate how true it is that God wants all men to be saved he went to great links to prepare a man to hear the gospel so he could be saved. He was an Ethiopian eunuch and a servant to the queen of Ethiopia. This Ethiopian eunuch was a person of great authority; he was the personal servant to the queen and he was in charge of her treasure. The Ethiopian had been to Jerusalem to worship God, but he had worshipped in the synagogue with the Jews and under the Law of Moses.

The eunuch and Phillip were far apart, and it was going to take some time and planning to get these two men together. The day before God had prepared the eunuch to hear the Word, he had prepared another man to teach him the Word; His name was Phillip. Phillip was told by the Spirit to meet the eunuch on the road as he was returning to Ethiopia. As the Ethiopian was returning from Jerusalem to his home he was reading the scriptures. It is interesting to know how he obtained a copy of God's Word, for they were very rare, but this just illustrates how much God wanted him to be saved. Luke wrote of this occasion.

> But an angel of the Lord spake unto Philip, saying, Arise, and go toward the south unto the way that goeth down from Jerusalem unto Gaza: the same is desert. And he arose and went: and behold, a man of Ethiopia, a eunuch of great authority under Candace, queen of the Ethiopians, who was over all her treasure, who had come to Jerusalem to worship; and he was returning and sitting in his chariot, and was reading the prophet Isaiah. And the Spirit said unto Philip, Go near, and join thyself to this chariot. And Philip ran to him, and heard him reading Isaiah the prophet, and said, Understandest thou what thou readest? And he said, How can I, except some one shall guide me? And he besought Philip to come up and sit with him. Now the passage of the Scripture which he was reading was this, He was led as a sheep to

> the slaughter; And as a lamb before his shearer is dumb, So he openeth not his mouth: In his humiliation his judgment was taken away: His generation who shall declare? For his life is taken from the earth. And the eunuch answered Philip, and said, I pray thee, of whom speaketh the prophet this? of himself, or of some other? And Philip opened his mouth, and beginning from this Scripture, preached unto him Jesus. And as they went on the way, they came unto a certain water; and the eunuch saith, Behold, here is water; what doth hinder me to be baptized? And Philip said, If thou believest with all thy heart, thou mayest. And he answered and said, I believe that Jesus Christ is the Son of God. And he commanded the chariot to stand still: and they both went down into the water, both Philip and the eunuch, and he baptized him. And when they came up out of the water, the Spirit of the Lord caught away Philip; and the eunuch saw him no more, for he went on his way rejoicing. (Acts 8:26-40)

The Ethiopian was a great man of high authority, but he was also a humble man to allow someone he met on the road to enter his chariot and become his instructor. When a person obeys the gospel they escape death and judgment and they enter the kingdom of God to live with their Master forever. To not obey the gospel is a tragic error. Paul wrote,

> ...and to you that are afflicted rest with us, at the revelation of the Lord Jesus from heaven with the angels of his power in flaming fire, rendering vengeance to them that know not God, and to them that obey not the gospel of our Lord Jesus: who

> shall suffer punishment, even eternal destruction from the face of the Lord and from the glory of his might when he shall come to be glorified in his saints, and to be marvelled at in all them that believed (because our testimony unto you was believed) in that day. (2 Thessalonians 1:7-10)

Peter wrote,

> For the time is come for judgment to begin at the house of God: and if it begin first at us, what shall be the end of them that obey not the gospel of God? And if the righteous is scarcely saved, where shall the ungodly and sinner appear? Wherefore let them also that suffer according to the will of God commit their souls in well-doing unto a faithful Creator. (1 Peter 4:17-19)

When Paul wrote his letter to the Romans he spoke of what men must do to avoid death, and what they must do to have life and enter the kingdom of God. He said the only death that comes without fear and is a pleasure to die is too die to sin, and as strange as it sounds, to death; and that is accomplished at baptism. Paul wrote,

> What shall we say then? Shall we continue in sin, that grace may abound? God forbid. We who died to sin, how shall we any longer live therein? Or are ye ignorant that all we who were baptized into Christ Jesus were baptized into his death? We were buried therefore with him through baptism unto death: that like as Christ was raised from the dead through the glory of the Father, so we also might walk in newness of life. For if we have

become united with him in the likeness of his death, we shall be also in the likeness of his resurrection; knowing this, that our old man was crucified with him, that the body of sin might be done away, that so we should no longer be in bondage to sin; for he that hath died is justified from sin. But if we died with Christ, we believe that we shall also live with him; knowing that Christ being raised from the dead dieth no more; death no more hath dominion over him. For the death that he died, he died unto sin once: but the life that he liveth, he liveth unto God. Even so reckon ye also yourselves to be dead unto sin, but alive unto God in Christ Jesus. Let not sin therefore reign in your mortal body, that ye should obey the lusts thereof: neither present your members unto sin as instruments of unrighteousness; but present yourselves unto God, as alive from the dead, and your members as instruments of righteousness unto God. For sin shall not have dominion over you: for ye are not under law, but under grace. What then? shall we sin, because we are not under law, but under grace? God forbid. Know ye not, that to whom ye present yourselves as servants unto obedience, his servants ye are whom ye obey; whether of sin unto death, or of obedience unto righteousness? But thanks be to God, that, whereas ye were servants of sin, ye became obedient from the heart to that form of teaching whereunto ye were delivered; and being made free from sin, ye became servants of righteousness. (Romans 6:1-18)

Paul wrote of a death that a man can chose to die, and if he does he escapes the eternal death that is punishment for sin; that death is the death a man dies when he is baptized, and it is a death he dies with Christ. Paul wrote,

> If ye died with Christ from the rudiments of the world, why, as though living in the world, do ye subject yourselves to ordinances Handle not, nor taste, nor touch (all which things are to perish with the using), after the precepts and doctrines of men? Which things have indeed a show of wisdom in will-worship, and humility, and severity to the body; but are not of any value against the indulgence of the flesh. (Colossians 2:20-23)

When a person dies with Christ at baptism he dies to an evil way of living; he dies to lasciviousness, lusts, winebibbing, reveling, carousing, and abominable idolatries and all evil ways (1 Peter 4:3).

A person must wonder why such a great phenomenon occurs at baptism, just being immersed in water, and why so many great and magnificent things happen when a person is baptized. In this world the people who witness a baptism see a person who had answered the Spirit's call to have their sins forgiven and become a member of God's family. They witness a person answering the question, "Do you believe that Jesus is the Christ, the Son of God and that he died on the cross to forgive your sins, and that he was resurrected from the tomb?" They say yes, I believe. That is called the good confession and it does not have to be asked in any certain words. Those who witness the event see a man who does the baptizing and a sinner who is going to be baptized going down into the water, and the sinner is completely immersed in the water. The two come up out of the water and the new man in Christ is congratulated for becoming a member of the church, for he has been born again.

However, if we could witness a baptism from the spiritual viewpoint, and see what happens in the spiritual world when a person is baptized, we would see a dead man who has heard the Word of God, he believes it, and he wants to obey it and live; he wants to obey the gospel. He stands before another man and he is asked to make the good confession. He does, and the dead man and the person who does the baptizing go down into the water, and the sinner is baptized. That dead man is buried in the water and he remains in that watery grave. Two living men vibrant with life come up out of the water, one having just been born anew, or born again into a new life in a spiritual world. The dead man who stays in the water no longer exists. The new man who is a Christian has just done what Jesus said a man must do to have spiritual life in the kingdom of God by being born again. John wrote,

> Now there was a man of the Pharisees, named Nicodemus, a ruler of the Jews: the same came unto him by night, and said to him, Rabbi, we know that thou art a teacher come from God; for no one can do these signs that thou doest, except God be with him. Jesus answered and said unto him, Verily, verily, I say unto thee, Except one be born anew, he cannot see the kingdom of God. Nicodemus saith unto him, How can a man be born when he is old? can he enter a second time into his mother's womb, and be born? Jesus answered, Verily, verily, I say unto thee, Except one be born of water and the Spirit, he cannot enter into the kingdom of God! That which is born of the flesh is flesh; and that which is of the Spirit is Spirit (John 1:1-6).

Paul explained clearly what it means for the old man to die with Christ and for a new man to be raised with Christ never to die again. He wrote,

> If ye died with Christ from the rudiments of the world, why, as though living in the world, do ye subject yourselves to ordinances, handle not, nor taste, nor touch (all which things are to perish with the using), after the precepts and doctrines of men? Which things have indeed a show of wisdom in will-worship, and humility, and severity to the body; but are not of any value against the indulgence of the flesh. If then ye were raised together with Christ, seek the things that are above, where Christ is, seated on the right hand of God. Set your mind on the things that are above, not on the things that are upon the earth. If then ye were raised together with Christ, seek the things that are above, where Christ is, seated on the right hand of God. Set your mind on the things that are above, not on the things that are upon the earth. For ye died, and your life is hid with Christ in God. When Christ, who is our life, shall be manifested, then shall ye also with him be manifested in glory. Put to death therefore your members which are upon the earth: fornication, uncleanness, passion, evil desire, and covetousness, which is idolatry; for which things' sake cometh the wrath of God upon the sons of disobedience: wherein ye also once walked, when ye lived in these things; but now do ye also put them all away: anger, wrath, malice, railing, shameful speaking out of your mouth: lie not one to another; seeing that ye have put off the old man with

> his doings, and have put on the new man, that is being renewed unto knowledge after the image of him that created him: where there cannot be Greek and Jew, circumcision and uncircumcision, barbarian, Scythian, bondman, freeman; but Christ is all, and in all. (Colossians 2:20-3:11)

Baptism is an event that should be considered the most important occurrence of a person's life, for without it a man dies in sin and he remains dead. But when the body of a person who has been baptized dies physically, and their sins have been washed away by the blood of Christ, they enter a new life to never have sin charged against them again. Then, one day when Christ comes again that body shall be resurrected to new life—if they walk in the light and keep the commandments of God. John wrote,

> And this is the message which we have heard from him and announce unto you, that God is light, and in him is no darkness at all. If we say that we have fellowship with him and walk in the darkness, we lie, and do not the truth: but if we walk in the light, as he is in the light, we have fellowship one with another, and the blood of Jesus his Son cleanseth us from all sin. If we say that we have no sin, we deceive ourselves, and the truth is not in us. If we confess our sins, he is faithful and righteous to forgive us our sins, and to cleanse us from all unrighteousness. (1 John 1:5-9)

There is joy in heaven when a person leaves sin and is baptized to have new life in Christ. Luke wrote, "I say unto you, that even so there shall be joy in heaven over one sinner that repenteth, more than over ninety and nine righteous persons, who need no repentance...even so, I say unto you, there is joy in the presence of the angels of God over one sinner that repenteth" (Luke 15:7, 10). There is joy amongst the angels because what pleases God pleases them, and should please us.

Can one even imagine having fellowship with the Almighty? In the Old Testament one could not even draw near to the Most Holy Place, the dwelling place of God, without being invited, and if one did, they died. But by the sacrifice of Christ we all become one family and we have fellowship with God. John wrote, "that which we have seen and heard declare we unto you also, that ye also may have fellowship with us: yea, and our fellowship is with the Father, and with his Son Jesus Christ: and these things we write, that our joy may be made full" (John 1:3-4).

When a person is a Christian and they make a mistake that is sinful, that sin it is not charged against them because they are instantly forgiven. John wrote, "Whosoever is begotten of God doeth no sin, because his seed abideth in him: and he cannot sin, because he is begotten of God" (1 John 3:9). The reason a person who is begotten of God cannot sin is because they are protected from sin by the blood of Christ. We know that Christians can sin and they do sin, but because they are walking in the light and trying not to sin, but they sin anyway, the sin is immediately washed away by the blood of Christ and it is not charged against the sinner, so it is the same as if he had not sinned.

CHAPTER 6

Christians Have Eternal Life in the New Resored World—It Is Called the Kingdom of God, the Kingdom of Heaven, and Abraham's Bosom

THE WORLD GOD CREATED for Adam and Eve and their children was perfect and beautiful; it could not be improved upon in any way. But there was a problem: it was a world that was controlled by law, and if the law was broken it would be defiled by sin, and it was. Adam and Eve lived under law, and if the law was broken the penalty for such misbehavior was death. Adam was given only one law to keep and so there was only one law he could break. It was a simple law at that: Adam was told not to eat of the fruit of God's holy tree. Adam broke the law and ate of the forbidden tree; he sinned and condemned himself and he died. His transgression also condemned his children and the creation. God redeemed the world that Adam defiled by the sacrifice of his Son, and He created a new world that was not under law and could not be defiled by sin, because it shall forever be protected by the blood of Jesus' cross. Paul wrote, "For sin shall not have dominion over you: for ye are not under law, but under grace" (Romans 6:14).

When a person lives under law and they sin, they die. When a person lives under grace and they sin, they can be forgiven. When a person lived under the Law of Moses and they sinned, they were immediately punished. To illustrate that, after Israel crossed the Jordan River to enter the land God promised them, the first city they came to was Jericho. It was the prime city of the Gentiles, and being the first city and the most glorious city in the land, everything in that city was devoted to God as holy. Joshua wrote,

> And the city shall be devoted, even it and all that is therein, to Jehovah: only Rahab the harlot shall live, she and all that are with her in the house, because she hid the messengers that we sent. But as for you, only keep yourselves from the devoted thing, lest when ye have devoted it, ye take of the devoted thing; so would ye make the camp of Israel accursed, and trouble it. But all the silver, and gold, and vessels of brass and iron, are holy unto Jehovah: they shall come into the treasury of Jehovah. (Joshua 6:17-19)

But there was a greedy man who disobeyed God's commandment and he stole several devoted items from Israel—and from God, and he sinned. Joshua wrote, "But the children of Israel committed a trespass in the devoted thing; for Achan, the son of Carmi, the son of Zabdi, the son of Zerah, of the tribe of Judah, took of the devoted thing: and the anger of Jehovah was kindled against the children of Israel" (Joshua 7:1). Achan's trespass was so severe that it caused the entire nation of Israel to be held guilty and to be punished for his trespass. His transgression stopped the entire nation of Israel in its tracks and thirty-six Israelites died fighting against a small village called Ai, and that small village should have been easily conquered. Joshua wrote,

> And Joshua sent men from Jericho to Ai, which is beside Beth-aven, on the east side of Beth-el, and spake unto them, saying, Go up and spy out the land. And the men went up and spied out Ai. And they returned to Joshua, and said unto him, Let not all the people go up; but let about two or three thousand men go up and smite Ai; make not all the people to toil thither; for they are but few. So there went up thither of the people about three thousand men: and they fled before the men of Ai. And the men of Ai smote of them about thirty and six men; and they chased them from before the gate even unto Shebarim, and smote them at the descent; and the hearts of the people melted, and became as water. And Joshua rent his clothes, and fell to the earth upon his face before the ark of Jehovah until the evening, he and the elders of Israel; and they put dust upon their heads. (Joshua 7:2-6)

From this we see what a serious crime it is to steal from God. Achan was quickly found out about what he had done and he was immediately punished for his transgression. Joshua wrote,

> And Joshua said, Why hast thou troubled us? Jehovah shall trouble thee this day. And all Israel stoned him with stones; and they burned them with fire, and stoned them with stones. And they raised over him a great heap of stones, unto this

> day; and Jehovah turned from the fierceness of his anger. Wherefore the name of that place was called, The valley of Achor, unto this day. (Joshua 7:25-26)

The wives and families of the thirty-six men who fell because of Achan's trespass were probably the first to pick up rocks to do away with the man who caused their death. It is possible to rob God. Anytime we take something from God that should be given to him, we rob Him. Malachi wrote,

> Will a man rob God? yet ye rob me. But ye say, Wherein have we robbed thee? In tithes and offerings. Ye are cursed with the curse; for ye rob me, even this whole nation. Bring ye the whole tithe into the store-house, that there may be food in my house, and prove me now herewith, saith Jehovah of hosts, if I will not open you the windows of heaven, and pour you out a blessing, that there shall not be room enough to receive it. And I will rebuke the devourer for your sakes, and he shall not destroy the fruits of your ground; neither shall your vine cast its fruit before the time in the field, saith Jehovah of hosts. (Malachi 3:8-11)

Today we see men who have committed grievous sins against God just as Achan had committed, and they live their lives out and are not punished until the day they die and they meet their judgment. That is the difference of being under law, and being under grace. When one is under law he is immediately held accountable for his transgression according to the law. When one is under grace God gives them time to repent. Paul wrote, "Or despisest thou the riches of his goodness and forbearance and longsuffering, not knowing that the goodness of God leadeth thee to repentance?" (Romans 2:4).

Christ achieved his goal in coming into the world to take away law, sin, and judgment— and establish grace, mercy, and righteousness. He also abolished death, both physical death and spiritual death, even though after he died on the cross many others died after him. But physical death can be considered abolished because of the resurrection, for it is by the resurrection that death just becomes a sleep (Acts 7:50). Jesus abolished physical death by the resurrection, and he abolished spiritual death—which is the separation of ones soul from God because of sin—and He gave the free gift of eternal life in its place. There are occasions when a gift not a "*free gift.*" There are times when a person gives a gift to someone and they expect something in return (that might be called politics—or a bribe). Paul wrote, "For the wages of sin is death; but the free gift of God is eternal life in Christ Jesus our Lord" (Romans 6:23). A wage is something a person earns and deserves; a free gift is something freely given as an act of kindness. Jesus abolished the wages of sin, which is death, by the way of the cross. Paul wrote,

> Be not ashamed therefore of the testimony of our Lord, nor of me his prisoner: but suffer hardship with the gospel according to the power of God; who saved us, and called us with a holy calling, not according to our works, but according to his own purpose and grace, which was given us in Christ Jesus before times eternal, but hath now been manifested by the appearing of our Saviour Christ Jesus, who abolished death, and brought life and immortality to light through the gospel. (2 Timothy 1:8-10)

When Jesus died on the cross he was separated from God to pay in full for all the consequences of sin and abolish death. Matthew wrote, "Now from the sixth hour there was darkness over all the land until the ninth hour. And about the ninth hour Jesus cried with a loud voice, saying, Eli, Eli, lama sabachthani? that is, My God, my God, why hast thou forsaken me?" (Matthew 27:45-46). Jesus died a physical death by being nailed to the cross and left there until he died. He died a spiritual death when He was forsaken by God and went into Hades, and He went to that dreadful place to take away the sins of the world. This was prophesied by the prophet Isaiah (Isaiah 53:10-12).

It was when Jesus was forsaken of God that His soul died, he was cut off out of the land of the living, and God saw the agony of his soul and was satisfied; His Son had paid the price in full to take away the sins of the world. The place other than the land of the living is the land of the dead.

What a price the Father paid to save His world from sin and death, and what a price the Son paid to abolish death and redeem the creation from its fall. Jesus died in such infinite trauma and agony that his death is indescribable, and he died for the transgressions others had committed.

Jesus replaced death and the fear of death with life and hope, for instead of God's children facing death they have been freely given the gift of eternal life. When Jesus abolished death he brought life and immortality to light through the gospel, and he also accomplished His purpose of redeeming the creation from its fallen state by restoring it to its formal glory—and greater. Luke prophesied of the time when that will transpire; it will be when Jesus comes again to restore all things and create the new heavens and the new earth. Until that time when Jesus comes again He will remain in heaven and rest there until the day of the resurrection, the day of new life, and the day of the new heaven and the new earth. Luke wrote,

> But the things which God foreshowed by the mouth of all the prophets, that his Christ should suffer, he thus fulfilled. Repent ye therefore, and turn again, that our sins may be blotted out, that so there may come seasons of refreshing from the presence of the Lord; and that he may send the Christ who hath been appointed for you, even Jesus: whom the heaven must receive until the times of restoration of all things, whereof God spake by the mouth of His holy prophets that have been from of old. (Acts 3:18-21)

The resurrection is an essential part of the cross, for if there is no resurrection the cross has no purpose. If Jesus died on the cross and was not raised from the tomb then he is no different than all the others who have died and remained dead. Paul wrote,

> Now if Christ is preached that he hath been raised from the dead, how say some among you that there is no resurrection of the dead? But if there is no resurrection of the dead, neither hath Christ been raised: and if Christ hath not been raised, then is our preaching vain, your faith also is vain. Yea, we are found false witnesses of God; because we witnessed of God that he raised up Christ: whom he raised not up, if so be that the dead are not raised. For if the dead are not raised, neither hath Christ been raised: and if Christ hath not been raised, your faith is vain; ye are yet in your sins. Then they also that are fallen asleep in Christ have perished. If we have only hoped in Christ in this life, we are of all men most pitiable. But now hath Christ been raised from the

> dead, the firstfruits of them that are asleep. For since by man came death, by man came also the resurrection of the dead. For as in Adam all die, so also in Christ shall all be made alive. But each in his own order: Christ the firstfruits; then they that are Christ's, at his coming. Then cometh the end, when he shall deliver up the kingdom to God, even the Father; when he shall have abolished all rule and all authority and power. For he must reign, till he hath put all his enemies under his feet. The last enemy that shall be abolished is death. For, He put all things in subjection under his feet. But when he saith, All things are put in subjection, it is evident that he is excepted who did subject all things unto him. And when all things have been subjected unto him, then shall the Son also himself be subjected to him that did subject all things unto him, that God may be all in all. (1 Corinthians 15:12-28)

After Jesus has finished all his work in this world the last thing He will do is deliver the kingdom of heaven up to the Almighty, and it is at that time all rule, authority, and power shall be abolished. The only power and authority that shall exist then shall be the power, the rule, and the authority of the Almighty. When Jesus was resurrected he was given all authority in heaven and on earth, and it was delegated authority given to him by his Father. After the resurrection of all the dead and the new heavens and the new earth are established (2 Peter 3:13), even the delegated authority that was given to Jesus by His Father shall be abolished, and Jesus shall again rule over all things, over heaven and earth; but not by delegated authority, it will be by His own inherent authority such as he had before he became the Son of man. That is the moment when Jesus shall deliver the kingdom of heaven up to his Father, and Jesus shall even deliver Himself and all his work up to the Father, and that is the moment when Jesus will no longer be the Son of God, He shall once again be Almighty Jehovah God as He was before he became a man, and God will be all in all.

There is coming the day when there will be a general resurrection of all the dead. That is the day the dead shall hear the voice of the archangel and the trump of God, and they shall leave their graves and live. John wrote, "Verily, verily, I say unto you, The hour cometh, and now is, when the dead shall hear the voice of the Son of God; and they that hear shall live" (John 5:25). Paul wrote,

> But we would not have you ignorant, brethren, concerning them that fall asleep; that ye sorrow not, even as the rest, who have no hope. For if we believe that Jesus died and rose again, even so them also that are fallen asleep in Jesus will God bring with him. For this we say unto you by the word of the Lord, that we that are alive, that are left unto the coming of the Lord, shall in no wise precede them that are fallen asleep. For the Lord himself shall descend from heaven, with a shout, with the voice of the archangel, and with the trump of God: and thc dcad in Christ shall rise first; then we that are alive, that are left, shall together with them be caught up in the clouds, to meet the Lord in the air: and so shall we ever be with the Lord. Wherefore comfort one another with these words. (1 Thessalonians 4:13-18)

Jesus proved beyond doubt that he had been raised from the tomb by appearing to his disciples and being with them for forty days. He also established the resurrection of all the dead as a certain event to come by his resurrection, and by raising someone who had died, such as Lazarus, and giving them life. Jesus had the power from his Father to speak and with his voice raise the dead. One such occasion was when a Roman centurion, a Gentile, had a servant whom he loved dearly, and his servant was very ill and at the point of death. Luke wrote,

> After he had ended all his sayings in the ears of the people, he entered into Capernaum. And a certain centurion's servant, who was dear unto him, was sick and at the point of death. And when he heard concerning Jesus, he sent unto him elders of the Jews, asking him that he would come and save his servant. And they, when they came to Jesus, besought him earnestly, saying, He is worthy that thou shouldest do this for him; for he loveth our nation, and himself built us our synagogue. And Jesus went with them. And when he was now not far from the house, the centurion sent friends to him, saying unto him, Lord, trouble not thyself; for I am not worthy that thou shouldest come under my roof: wherefore neither thought I myself worthy to come unto thee: but say the word, and my servant shall be healed. For I also am a man set under authority, having under myself soldiers: and I say to this one, Go, and he goeth; and to another, Come, and he cometh; and to my servant, Do this, and he doeth it. And when Jesus heard these things, he marvelled at him, and turned and said unto the multitude that followed him, I say unto you, I have not found so great faith, no, not in Israel. And they that were sent, returning to the house, found the servant whole. (Luke 7:1-10)

The centurion was an amazing and humble man of high authority. He was the commander of one hundred men, Roman soldiers, and he loved each one of them dearly. He had heard of Christ and what he had done for others, and when one of his servants was sick he sent for him to heal his servant. Here is a man of repute who sent a servant to the Christ to ask him for help because he felt so inferior to him he felt uncomfortable just being in his presence, and he would not approach Jesus himself. The centurion knew about authority; when he gave a command it was obeyed, and He knew when Jesus gave a command, like calling a dead man out of his grave, he had the authority to know that his word would also be obeyed. Jesus said He had never seen such faith, not even in all of Israel. Jesus just spoke and healed the centurion's servant.

It was not long after Jesus had healed the centurion's servant that another person, a widow needed his help. Luke wrote,

> And it came to pass soon afterwards, that he went to a city called Nain; and his disciples went with him, and a great multitude. Now when he drew near to the gate of the city, behold, there was carried out one that was dead, the only son of his mother, and she was a widow: and much people of the city was with her. And when the Lord saw her, he had compassion on her, and said unto her, Weep not. And he came nigh and touched the bier: and the bearers stood still. And he said, Young man, I say unto thee, Arise. And he that was dead sat up, and began to speak. And he gave him to his mother. And fear took hold on all: and they glorified God, saying, A great prophet is arisen among us: and, God hath visited his people. And this report went forth concerning him in the whole of Judaea, and all the region round about.

> And the disciples of John told him of all these things. And John calling unto him two of his disciples sent them to the Lord, saying, Art thou he that cometh, or look we for another? And when the men were come unto him, they said, John the Baptist hath sent us unto thee, saying, Art thou he that cometh, or look we for another? In that hour he cured many of diseases and plagues and evil spirits; and on many that were blind he bestowed sight. And he answered and said unto them, Go and tell John the things which ye have seen and heard; the blind receive their sight, the lame walk, the lepers are cleansed, and the deaf hear, the dead are raised up, the poor have good tidings preached to them. And blessed is he, whosoever shall find no occasion of stumbling in me. (Luke 7:11-23)

John the Baptist was not well pleased with what Jesus was doing, for he, just like the rest of the Jews, thought Jesus had come to restore the nation of Israel to its formal glory and the Jews would rule the world. They believed that up to the time Jesus left this world and ascended into heaven. Luke wrote,

> "...and, being assembled together with them, he charged them not to depart from Jerusalem, but to wait for the promise of the Father, which, said he, ye heard from me: for John indeed baptized with water; but ye shall be baptized in the Holy Spirit not many days hence. They therefore, when they were come together, asked him, saying, Lord, dost thou at this time restore the kingdom to Israel? And he said unto them, It is not for

> you to know times or seasons, which the Father hath set within His own authority. (Acts 2:4-7)

The widow of Nain was in serious need, she and her son could function well working together to take care of themselves and their needs, but the widow alone would have a very difficult and lonely time living without her son. When Jesus saw the woman stricken with grief and in great mourning, he went to her aid and immediately ended her sorrow by raising her son from the bier. She had her son back, something she never dreamed possible. Jesus cared about the grief and problems people had, and he did what he could to help them and relieve their misery. He still feels the same way about his children today, he might not be here on earth but he can help is in our problems, even when he is in heaven, and we are here in this world.

Then there came a time when a Jew needed Jesus' help to heal his daughter. He was an important man for he was the ruler of a synagogue. The Jewish people who worshipped in the synagogues and kept the Law of Moses were not fond of Christians who taught that the Law of Moses had been fulfilled and was no longer in force. The Pharisees, who were strong members of the synagogues, were the very ones who wanted to kill Jesus, and eventually they did. But Jairus was willing to give up all his prejudices against the Christians and their Leader if he would save his daughter. He went to the Christ and fell at his feet and begged him for help, for Jesus was the only man who had the power to heal his daughter. Mark wrote,

> And there cometh one of the rulers of the synagogue, Jairus by name; and seeing him, he falleth at his feet, and beseecheth him much, saying, My little daughter is at the point of death: I pray thee, that thou come and lay thy hands on her, that she may be made whole, and live. And he went with

> him; and a great multitude followed him, and they thronged him... While he yet spake, they come from the ruler of the synagogue's house saying, Thy daughter is dead: why troublest thou the Teacher any further? But Jesus, not heeding the word spoken, saith unto the ruler of the synagogue, Fear not, only believe. And he suffered no man to follow with him, save Peter, and James, and John the brother of James. And they come to the house of the ruler of the synagogue; and he beholdeth a tumult, and many weeping and wailing greatly. And when he was entered in, he saith unto them, Why make ye a tumult, and weep? the child is not dead, but sleepeth. And they laughed him to scorn. But he, having put them all forth, taketh the father of the child and her mother and them that were with him, and goeth in where the child was. And taking the child by the hand, he saith unto her, Talitha cumi; which is, being interpreted, Damsel, I say unto thee, Arise. And straightway the damsel rose up, and walked; for she was twelve years old. And they were amazed straightway with a great amazement. And he charged them much that no man should know this: and he commanded that something should be given her to eat. (Mark 5:22-24, 35-43)

There was another man Jesus raised from the tomb, his name was Lazarus. Of all those who Jesus raised from death to life Lazarus is the one most remembered, for Lazarus and Jesus were good friends. John is the apostle who wrote of Lazarus' resurrection.

Now a certain man was sick, Lazarus of Bethany, of the village of Mary and her sister Martha. And it was that Mary who anointed the Lord with ointment, and wiped his feet with her hair, whose brother Lazarus was sick. The sisters therefore sent unto him, saying, Lord, behold, he whom thou lovest is sick. But when Jesus heard it, he said, This sickness is not unto death, but for the glory of God, that the Son of God may be glorified thereby. Now Jesus loved Martha, and her sister, and Lazarus. When therefore he heard that he was sick, he abode at that time two days in the place where he was. Then after this he saith to the disciples, Let us go into Judaea again. The disciples say unto him, Rabbi, the Jews were but now seeking to stone thee; and goest thou thither again? Jesus answered, Are there not twelve hours in the day? If a man walk in the day, he stumbleth not, because he seeth the light of this world. But if a man walk in the night, he stumbleth, because the light is not in him. These things spake he: and after this he saith unto them, Our friend Lazarus is fallen asleep; but I go, that I may awake him out of sleep. The disciples therefore said unto him, Lord, if he is fallen asleep, he will recover. Now Jesus had spoken of his death: but they thought that he spake of taking rest in sleep. Then Jesus therefore said unto them plainly, Lazarus is dead. And I am glad for your sakes that I was not there, to the intent ye may believe; nevertheless let us go unto him. Thomas therefore, who is called Didymus, said unto his fellow-disciples, Let us also go, that we may die with him. So when Jesus came, he found that he had been in the tomb four days already. Now Bethany was nigh unto Jerusalem, about fifteen furlongs off; and many of the Jews had come to Martha and Mary, to console them concerning their brother. Martha therefore, when she heard that Jesus was coming, went and met him: but Mary still sat in the house. Martha therefore said unto Jesus, Lord, if thou hadst been here, my brother had not died. And even now I know that, whatsoever thou shalt ask of God, God will give thee. Jesus saith unto her, Thy brother shall rise again. Martha saith unto him, I know that he shall rise again in the resurrection at the last day. Jesus said unto her, I am the resurrection, and the life: he that believeth on me, though he die, yet shall he live; and whosoever liveth and believeth on me shall never die. Believest thou this? She saith unto him, Yea, Lord: I have believed that thou art the Christ, the Son of God, even he that cometh into the world. And when she had said this, she went away, and called Mary her sister secretly, saying, The Teacher is her, and calleth thee. And she, when she heard it, arose quickly, and went unto him. (Now Jesus was not yet come into the village, but was still in the place where Martha met him.) The Jews then who were with her in the house, and were consoling her, when they saw Mary, that she rose up quickly and went out, followed her, supposing that she was going unto the tomb to weep there. Mary therefore, when she came where Jesus was, and saw him, fell down at his feet, saying unto him, Lord, if thou hadst been here, my brother had not died. When Jesus therefore saw her weeping, and the Jews also weeping who came with her, he groaned in the spirit, and was troubled, and said, Where have ye laid him? They say unto him, Lord, come and see. Jesus wept. The Jews therefore said, Behold how he loved him! But some of them said, Could not this man, who opened the eyes of him that was blind, have caused that this man also should not die? Jesus therefore again groaning in himself cometh to the tomb. Now it was a cave, and a stone lay against it. Jesus saith, Take ye away the stone. Martha, the sister of him that was dead, saith unto him, Lord, by this time the body decayeth; for he hath been dead four days. Jesus saith unto her, Said I not unto thee, that, if thou believedst, thou shouldest see the glory of God? So they took away the stone. And Jesus lifted up his eyes, and said, Father, I thank thee that thou heardest me. And I knew that thou hearest me always: but because of the multitude that standeth around I said it, that they may believe that thou didst send me. And when he had thus spoken, he cried with a loud voice, Lazarus, come forth. He that was dead came forth, bound hand and foot with grave-clothes; and his face was bound about with a napkin. Jesus saith unto them, Loose him, and let him go. Many therefore of the Jews, who came to Mary and beheld that which he did, believed on him. But some of them went away to the Pharisees, and told them the things which Jesus had done. The chief priests therefore and the Pharisees gathered a council, and said, What do we? for this man doeth many signs. If we let him thus alone, all men will believe on him: and the Romans will come and take away both our place and our nation. (John 11:1-48)

Jesus was a dear friend to Lazarus and his sisters Mary and Martha. When Lazarus became very ill his sisters sent for Jesus, they wanted him to heal their brother. Jesus waited for Lazarus to die before he would return to Bethany, he did not want to heal Lazarus, He wanted to raise him from death that by bringing him back to life so the Son and his Father would be glorified. Jesus and his disciples returned to Bethany, he met Mary, and the first thing she said to Jesus was, if you had been here my brother would not have died. A few moments later he met Martha, and he heard those same words. Then the entire company joined in and said that if Jesus had been there Lazarus would still be alive. They blamed Jesus for Lazarus' death. They knew Jesus had the power to heal Lazarus, but they did not even think about him having the power to raise him from the dead.

All the family and friends of Lazarus were gravely mourning and weeping, and that had an effect on Jesus. His Spirit became very sad, not because of Lazarus for he knew in a few moments Lazarus would live again; He grieved with His friends because their feelings of sorrow were contagious, and Jesus wept. Jesus also wept over a dead city, Bethphage and Bethany (Luke 19:29, 41).

Jesus was taken to Lazarus' tomb and told his friends to open the grave. They refused as Lazarus had been dead too long in a hot climate. They opened it and Jesus said with a loud voice, "Lazarus, come forth." Lazarus lived again but he had to have his sisters remove his grave clothes and the napkin that covered his face. It was wise of Jesus to say, "Lazarus, come forth," for if he had said "Come forth" it is possible there would not have been a grave in the cemetery with a body remaining in it.

Jesus, Lazarus, and his sisters were very close friends and they were together often (John 12:1-2). Lazarus became so famous that the chief priests thought he was making Jesus a little too popular, and the Jews wanted to kill him. John wrote, "The common people therefore of the Jews learned that he was there:

and they came, not for Jesus' sake only, but that they might see Lazarus also, whom he had raised from the dead. But the chief priests took counsel that they might put Lazarus also to death; because that by reason of him many of the Jews went away, and believed on Jesus" (John 12:9-11).

We do not know what happened to any of these people after they had been raised from the dead. There is no record of any of them remembering their resurrection or what happened to them when after they had been raised from death.

There was one man who died and he did tell of his experience and what happened to him while he was dead. His name was Paul. Paul and Barnabus were on their first missionary journey and they went to a city called Lystra. Luke wrote,

> And at Lystra there sat a certain man, impotent in his feet, a cripple from his mother's womb, who never had walked. The same heard Paul speaking, who, fastening eyes upon him, and seeing that he had faith to be made whole, said with a loud voice, Stand upright on thy feet. And he leaped up and walked. And when the multitude saw what Paul had done, they lifted up their voice, saying in the speech of Lycaonia, The gods are come down to us in the likeness of men. And they called Barnabas, Jupiter; and Paul, Mercury, because he was the chief speaker. (Acts 14:8-12)

Neither Paul nor Barnabas would tolerate such nonsense and they tried to put an end to it as quickly as possible. Luke wrote,

> But when the apostles, Barnabas and Paul heard of it, they rent their garments, and sprang forth among the multitude, crying out and saying, Sirs, why do ye these things? We also are men of

> like passions with you, and bring you good tidings, that ye should turn from these vain things unto a living God, who made the heaven and the earth and the sea, and all that in them is:.." (Acts 14:14-15)

It was only a matter of hours that the Jews had heard of Paul's success and they went to Lystra and convinced the people that Paul was an evil man and he should be stoned. Luke wrote, "But there came Jews thither from Antioch and Iconium: and having persuaded the multitudes, they stoned Paul, and dragged him out of the city, supposing that he was dead" (Acts 14:19). It is difficult to imagine two men whose works were so great the citizens in the city thought they must be gods and wanted to worship them, and the next day consider them criminals guilty of a capital crime, for which Paul was stoned.

Paul died in the stoning, for no person ever survived a Jewish stoning. Large stones, larger than grapefruit were hurled at the victim until his head was crushed and his body broken in pieces, and the victim lay on the ground a bloody mess completely covered with rocks. Such was Paul's fate. But Paul did not remain dead; he came back to life not long after he was stoned. Proof of this is, when the time was right Paul rose up out of his rock pile and walked out of it as if nothing had happened, and one does not do that after they had been stoned. The Lord brought Paul back to life because there was still much for him to do. The next day, after his stoning, he and Barnabas walked some thirty miles to the town of Derbe to do their work there. Paul had no broken bones or even bruises as the Lord healed him to keep on keeping on. It is no less a miracle that Paul left his rock pile and walked over thirty miles the next day than for him to have been raised from the dead. Luke wrote,

> But as the disciples stood round about him, he rose up, and entered into the city: and on the morrow he went forth with Barnabas to Derbe. And when they had preached the gospel to that city, and had made many disciples, they returned to Lystra, and to Iconium, and to Antioch, confirming the souls of the disciples, exhorting them to continue in the faith, and that through many tribulations we must enter into the kingdom of God. (Luke 14:20-22)

But something miraculous happened to Paul when he died. Paul said,

> I must needs glory, though it is not expedient; but I will come to visions and revelations of the Lord. I know a man in Christ, fourteen years ago (whether in the body, I know not; or whether out of the body, I know not; God knoweth), such a one caught up even to the third heaven. And I know such a man (whether in the body, or apart from the body, I know not; God knoweth), how that he was caught up into Paradise, and heard unspeakable words, which it is not lawful for a man to utter. On behalf of such a one will I glory: but on mine own behalf I will not glory, save in my weaknesses. For if I should desire to glory, I shall not be foolish; for I shall speak the truth: but I forbear, lest any man should account of me above that which he seeth me to be, or heareth from me. And by reason of the exceeding greatness of the revelations, that I should not be exalted overmuch, there was given to me a thorn in the flesh. (2 Corinthians 12:1-7)

The vision Paul had was so real and so remarkable that he spoke of what happened to him in the third person; he would not allow having such an infinite experience to even be associated with him. We know that it was Paul speaking of himself having the vision because he was the one who was given the thorn in the flesh to not allow him to be over exalted. Paul was allowed to enter the third heaven, and that is the holy dwelling place of the Almighty. Then he entered Paradise where the spirits of the saints go when their spirits leave their bodies. Paul's experience was completely spiritual, for flesh and blood cannot enter heaven (1 Corinthians 15:50).

Part of Jesus' work in abolishing the death of his children was to also abolish the death the creation suffered, for when it fell because of sin, it died. Paul wrote,

> For I reckon that the sufferings of this present time are not worthy to be compared with the glory which shall be revealed to us-ward. For the earnest expectation of the creation waiteth for the revealing of the sons of God. For the creation was subjected to vanity, not of its own will, but by reason of him who subjected it, in hope that the creation itself also shall be delivered from the bondage of corruption into the liberty of the glory of the children of God. For we know that the whole creation groaneth and travaileth in pain together until now. And not only so, but ourselves also, who have the first-fruits of the Spirit, even we ourselves groan within ourselves, waiting for our adoption, to wit, the redemption of our body. For in hope were we saved: but hope that is seen is not hope: for who hopeth for that which he seeth? But if we hope for that which we see not,

> then do we with patience wait for it. (Romans 8:18-25)

After Jesus had finished his ministry in this present evil world, as Paul called it (Galatians 1:4), he met with his apostles on a mountain. It was on the mount that Jesus gave the apostles the Great Commission and instructed them in what they were to do when he left. Matthew wrote of that occasion.

> But the eleven disciples went into Galilee, unto the mountain where Jesus had appointed them. And when they saw him, they worshipped him; but some doubted. And Jesus came to them and spake unto them, saying, All authority hath been given unto me in heaven and on earth. Go ye therefore, and make disciples of all the nations, baptizing them into the name of the Father and of the Son and of the Holy Spirit: teaching them to observe all things whatsoever I commanded you: and lo, I am with you always, even unto the end of the world. (Matthew 28:16-20)

It is interesting that Jesus said all authority had been given to Him in heaven and on earth—that is all authority over everything. If Jesus is God wouldn't he inherently have all authority? Yes, but when he gave up his equality with God he also emptied himself of that authority. But when Jesus had finished his work of redemption God gave him back that authority, and it was delegated authority given to him as a man. It is the Man, Jesus, who is the King of kings and the Lord of lords who rules and controls the universe, and he does it by the delegated authority His Father gave him as a man.

Even after Jesus had been with his apostles for forty days, and they saw him, heard him, touched Him, and ate with him, some doubted. The resurrection was so astonishing that at first even the apostles refused to believe it was real. Mark wrote,

> Now when he was risen early on the first day of the week, he appeared first to Mary Magdalene, from whom he had cast out seven demons. She went and told them that had been with him, as they mourned and wept. And they, when they heard that he was alive, and had been seen of her, disbelieved. And after these things he was manifested in another form unto two of them, as they walked, on their way into the country. And they went away and told it unto the rest: neither believed they them. And afterward he was manifested unto the eleven themselves as they sat at meat; and he upbraided them with their unbelief and hardness of heart, because they believed not them that had seen him after he was risen. And he said unto them, Go ye into all the world, and preach the gospel to the whole creation. He that believeth and is baptized shall be saved; but he that disbelieveth shall be condemned. (Mark 16:9-16)

Luke also wrote of how difficult it was to convince His disciples, even the chosen apostles that the Man whom they knew to be the Son of God was no longer in the tomb, but he had risen and was alive and well. The women whom Jesus had taught did not believe he had risen. On the third day, the day Jesus taught his disciples that he would no longer be in the tomb, several women went to the tomb to anoint his body. When they arrived at the tomb they saw the stone covering the grave had been moved. They entered the tomb and there was no body in it. They thought the body had been moved or stolen, but a resurrection did not enter their minds. John wrote,

> Now on the first day of the week cometh Mary Magdalene early, while it was yet dark, unto the tomb, and seeth the stone taken away from the tomb. She runneth therefore, and cometh to Simon Peter, and to the other disciple whom Jesus loved, and saith unto them, They have taken away the Lord out of the tomb, and we know not where they have laid him. Peter therefore went forth, and the other disciple, and they went toward the tomb. And they ran both together: and the other disciple outran Peter, and came first to the tomb; and stooping and looking in, he seeth the linen cloths lying; yet entered he not in. Simon Peter therefore also cometh, following him, and entered into the tomb; and he beholdeth the linen cloths lying, and the napkin, that was upon his head, not lying with the linen cloths, but rolled up in a place by itself. Then entered in therefore the other disciple also, who came first to the tomb, and he saw, and believed. For as yet they knew not the scripture, that he must rise from the dead. (John 20:1-9)

When Jesus was made alive He did not remove His grave clothes, He just vanished out of them and left them on the place where his disciples had laid him, and he was in no hurry. He took His face covering and neatly rolled it up and placed it on a shelf by itself. Luke wrote,

> But on the first day of the week, at early dawn, they came unto the tomb, bringing the spices

> which they had prepared. And they found the stone rolled away from the tomb. And they entered in, and found not the body of the Lord Jesus. And it came to pass, while they were perplexed thereabout, behold, two men stood by them in dazzling apparel: and as they were affrighted and bowed down their faces to the earth, they said unto them, Why seek ye the living among the dead? He is not here, but is risen: remember how he spake unto you when he was yet in Galilee, saying that the Son of man must be delivered up into the hands of sinful men, and be crucified, and the third day rise again. And they remembered his words, and returned from the tomb, and told all these things to the eleven, and to all the rest. Now they were Mary Magdalene, and Joanna, and Mary the mother of James: and the other women with them told these things unto the apostles. And these words appeared in their sight as idle talk; and they disbelieved them. (Luke 24:1-11)

It is interesting that on the Sunday morning Jesus was resurrected several women went to the tomb to anoint His body, but Mary, the mother of Jesus was not with them. Why? Jesus must have talked to Mary quite often about many things; things she would want to know. She would want to know why God had chosen her to be his mother. She would also want to know why her Son, the Son of God, had come into this world and what his mission would be. Jesus must have explained to Mary very clearly about how he would end his life by being crucified. Jesus prepared Mary very well for what she had to witness—the day of the cross. That must have been the reason Mary could watch them crucify her Son and endure it, and maintain her sanity. She knew that her Son had been sent to be the Savior of the world, and for that to be accomplished it all had to be done God's way, and that meant Jesus must die by being crucified. Just as Jesus told Mary about how he would die, by crucifixion, he also instructed her about how he would be resurrected from the grave only three days after his crucifixion.

Mary believed all the things Jesus had told her about many things. Luke wrote, "And he went down with them, and came to Nazareth; and he was subject unto them: and his mother kept all these sayings in her heart. And Jesus advanced in wisdom and stature, and in favor with God and men" (Luke 2:51-52). One of the things Jesus taught Mary was how severe the day of the cross would be so she could be prepared for what she must witness. He also told her that he would be raised from the dead on the third day, and on that day he would no longer be in the tomb. That is why Mary was not with the women who went to the tomb to anoint Jesus' body—she knew that there would not be any body in that tomb to anoint.

Joseph, Jesus' father on the other hand died somewhere between the year Jesus was twelve and the time he began his ministry, because the last mention of Jesus' father is recorded in Luke 2:40–52. That was the time when Jesus had stayed behind in the temple and had amazed the doctors of the law with his questions and answers. At that young age Jesus knew who he was—the Son of God—and he knew who his real Father was, and what his Father's business was: Salvation! He knew what his purpose in life would be. However, Joseph never saw Jesus accomplish his mission. When Jesus went to the cross Joseph was not there, for he had died. I believe God took Joseph home to heaven before Jesus went to the cross for a reason. God knew that the cross was a burden that Joseph could not endure to witness—that is, seeing his Son spit on and so terribly abused and then nailed to the cross, lifted up, and left to die. Joseph, going home to be with God was an act of great mercy on God's part to spare him from seeing his beloved Son being crucified. Isaiah wrote, "The righteous perisheth, and no man layeth it to heart; and merciful men are taken away, none considering that the righteous is taken away from the evil to come. He entereth into peace; they rest in their beds, each one that walketh in his uprightness" (Isaiah 57:1–2). God knew Joseph could never withstand the grief, the misery, the pain, and the agony that would come with seeing such a terrible thing happen to his beloved Son whom he loved dearly. Mary did bear that burden, but Jesus had prepared her well for what she must witness. It has been said that women can bear grief and heartbreak much better than men can.

What a day it will be when Jesus comes again all the dead shall be raised from their graves. They shall witness this world's disappearance by it being burned with fire so intense it will dissolve everything God made, and the new heavens and the new earth will take its place. All the living on earth that have not died shall also see all these glorious things. Peter wrote,

> Knowing this first, that in the last days mockers shall come with mockery, walking after their own lusts, and saying, Where is the promise of his coming? for, from the day that the fathers fell asleep, all things continue as they were from the beginning of the creation. For this they willfully forget, that there were heavens from of old, and an earth compacted out of water and amidst water, by the word of God; by which means the world that then was, being overflowed with water, perished: but the heavens that now are, and the earth, by the same word have been stored up for fire, being reserved against the day of judgment and destruction of ungodly men. But forget not this one thing, beloved, that one day is with the Lord as a thousand years, and a thousand years as one day. The Lord is not slack concerning his promise, as

some count slackness; but is longsuffering to you-ward, not wishing that any should perish, but that all should come to repentance. But the day of the Lord will come as a thief; in the which the heavens shall pass away with a great noise, and the elements shall be dissolved with fervent heat, and the earth and the works that are therein shall be burned up. Seeing that these things are thus all to be dissolved, what manner of persons ought ye to be in all holy living and godliness, looking for and earnestly desiring the coming of the day of God, by reason of which the heavens being on fire shall be dissolved, and the elements shall melt with fervent heat? But, according to his promise, we look for new heavens and a new earth, wherein dwelleth righteousness. Wherefore, beloved, seeing that ye look for these things, give diligence that ye may be found in peace, without spot and blameless in his sight. And account that the long-suffering of our Lord is salvation; even as our beloved brother Paul also, according to the wisdom given to him, wrote unto you. (2 Peter 3:4-15)

Conclusion

DEATH AND EVEN THE fear of death have been abolished by Christ; it was eliminated by his cross and by his resurrection. Therefore in the Christian world death does not exist. Since there is no such thing as death in kingdom of God then there should not bc any fcar of death, it is unreasonable to fear something that doesn't exist. When on the third day of Jesus' crucifixion Jesus was raised from the tomb by the power of His Father, exactly as he taught throughout his ministry he would be, he proved once for all that death has been conquered. In the letter to the Hebrews it is written, "Since then the children are sharers in flesh and blood, he also himself in like manner partook of the same; that through death he might bring to nought him that had the power of death, that is, the devil; and might deliver all them who through fear of death were all their lifetime subject to bondage" (Hebrews 2:14-15). Christians are no longer in bondage to death or the fear of death because Jesus bore that fear for them, for Jesus dreadfully feared the death he was about to face. He died it anyway, and because he died He abolished death for his children. When Jesus was in the garden of Gethsemane preparing himself for the cross he asked his Father three times to find a way for him to escape the cup he was close to having to drink. Mark wrote,

> And they come unto a place which was named Gethsemane: and he saith unto his disciples, Sit ye here, while I pray. And he taketh with him Peter and James and John, and began to be greatly amazed, and sore troubled. And he saith unto them, My soul is exceeding sorrowful even unto death: abide ye here, and watch. And he went forward a little, and fell on the ground, and prayed that, if it were possible, the hour might pass away from him. And he said, Abba, Father, all things are possible unto thee; remove this cup from me: howbeit not what I will, but what thou wilt. (Mark 14:32-36)

What agony it caused Jesus' Father to hear that prayer from His only begotten Son—knowing that he must deny his request and let him suffer and die.

There is a way for Christians to live a very happy and secure life. That way is to arise in the morning, thank the Father for the day, and press on with it doing the things that need to be done and enjoying the things they like to do, trusting the Father to care of them and to answer their prayers. (George Burns said when he arose in the morning the first thing he did was read the newspaper, and the first thing he looked at were the obituaries; if he wasn't in them he pressed on with his day). At the end of the day when a person retires it is nice to thank the Father for the day and look forward to the next. When a person knows that they are coming close to ending their life in this world it causes their faith in the Almighty to become even stronger, and they should not dread it as a fearful thing, but to accept it as the way out of a world where death, evil, and unhappiness are prominent and entrance into a new world where life, righteousness, and contentment are the way of the living, and that is the way their new world will be forever.

Not everyone must be a preacher or a teacher to be a Christian. To become a Christian one must obey the gospel and live the Christian life, and there are many occupations one can have and live that life. There was a salesman who felt he wanted to better his life and be a preacher of the Word. He quit his job in sales and attended a conservative Bible school to prepare for his new life. As the new class started in their first day of school, the class initiation, the students were questioned to find out how well they knew the Bible. The teacher asked the class, "what is a prophet?" The salesman student answered, "That's when you sell it for more than you paid for it and you make money." The class was asked, "What is the Great Commission?" Again that student said, "Fifty percent."

El Fin

www.ingramcontent.com/pod-product-compliance
Lightning Source LLC
LaVergne TN
LVHW050650100826
845148LV00011B/2057

* 9 7 8 1 6 3 3 5 7 4 8 1 6 *